Barnsley House and Garden.

Shire County Guide 32

GLOUCESTERSHIRE

Peter Stanier

Shire Publications Ltd

CONTENTS

Printed in Great Britain by C. I. Thomas & Sons (Haverfordwest) Ltd, Press Buildings, Merlins Bridge, Haverfordwest, Dyfed SA61 1XF.

British Library Cataloguing in Publication Data: Stanier, Peter. Gloucestershire. – (Shire County Guide, 32). 1. Gloucestershire – Visitors' guides. I. Title. 914. 24104858. ISBN 0-7478-0110-X.

ACKNOWLEDGEMENTS
The following illustrations are acknowledged to Cadbury Lamb: cover, title page and those on pages 5, 7, 8, 9, 10, 15, 16, 23, 25, 26 (bottom), 28 (bottom), 30, 32, 33, 34, 35, 36, 38, 39, 42, 43, 44, 46, 49, 51, 55 (bottom), 57, 59, 60, 62 (right),63, 65, 67, 69, 70, 71, 73, 74 and 75. All the remaining photographs are by the author. The map was prepared by Robert Dizon.

Cover: *Arlington Row, Bibury.*

Below: *The Long Canal and the Tall Pavilion, Westbury Court Garden.*

The famous Severn bore attracts onlookers at vantage points along the riverbank.

1
Gloucestershire

Gloucestershire lies astride the Severn's great funnel-like estuary, which is such a distinguishing feature on the map of Britain. The old county reached south almost to Bristol and Bath, but this area was lost to the new county of Avon in 1974. It now covers an area of 1030 square miles (2668 square km) and has a population of around half a million. The main centres are Gloucester, which grew at the lowest crossing point of the Severn into Wales, and the relatively recent spa town of Cheltenham. Other centres are Cirencester and Stroud, with many much smaller towns throughout.

Gloucestershire has three main regions. The limestone Cotswold Hills are the most extensive and best known, covering the east of the county from Wotton-under-Edge in the south to Chipping Campden in the north. Much of this region is a high plateau dissected by streams, rising at times to over 1000 feet (305 metres). The Cotswold Edge drops sharply to the west, and at its foot lies the Severn Vale, on the flood plain of the lower Severn and its estuary. The much smaller Forest of Dean is

the third region, hemmed in between the Severn and the lower Wye valley, which makes the boundary with Wales. Beneath this royal forest are Carboniferous limestones, sandstones and coal measures. The drainage of Gloucestershire is associated with Britain's two longest rivers, the Severn and the Thames. The former dominates the west and, with two exceptions, all the main Cotswold rivers flow gently south-east towards the Thames, which has its source near Cirencester.

Into this landscape came early man. In neolithic times Crickley Hill was a key centre, while settlements elsewhere in the Cotswolds are attested by the many examples of chambered long barrows of this period. By the iron age this was the territory of the Dobunni, who built some excellent hillforts along the Cotswold Edge. Gloucestershire was important in Roman times, when Cirencester was the second largest town in Britain. Gloucester was also large, a *colonia* at a vital crossing point on the Severn. Traces of small towns and many villas, such as Chedworth, have been found in the Cotswolds, undoubtedly related to the farming of this good land. Temples were built at Lydney and Littledean on the edge of the Forest of Dean, a district where the Romans were mining iron ore and perhaps coal. The Roman road system has left its mark in the modern road pattern, especially the famous Fosse Way and Ermine Way which meet at Cirencester.

The Saxon advance into Gloucestershire was largely complete by the late sixth century AD. Offa's Dyke was built by the king of Mercia in the late eighth century as a boundary with Wales. Offa also founded a nunnery at Winchcombe in about AD 787, the site later becoming an important abbey. Gloucester was a place of some importance by the late ninth century, after a Mercian palace was established at Kingsholm. In AD 909 Ethelfleda founded St Oswald's Priory here at *Gleawcester*, which was refortified as a burh with a mint. Deerhurst was the main monastery of the kingdom of Hwicce, and it was here beside the Severn that Edmund Ironside and Canute made a treaty in 1016, dividing England between the Saxons and Danes. After the Norman conquest, William I was staying at Gloucester when he decided to carry out the Domesday survey.

The county is conspicuous in its richness of Saxon and Norman churches. Abbeys were founded at Cirencester, Gloucester, Hailes, Kingswood, Tewkesbury and Winchcombe. While some were places of pilgrimage, their wealth was based mostly on the wool trade, for which the Cotswolds were renowned in the middle ages. Although a recent foundation, Prinknash Abbey near Gloucester continues the monastic tradition today. There are few castles in the county, and Berkeley, Beverston, St Briavels and Sudeley are the best remaining examples. Traces of Gloucester's castle have long since vanished, while earthworks are often all that survive of others. Thornbury Castle, the Duke of Buckingham's Tudor home, is now in the county of Avon.

Henry III was crowned at Gloucester Abbey (now the cathedral), while a century later Edward II was brutally murdered at Berkeley Castle in 1327. His body was buried at the abbey, where it became a shrine for pilgrims. In 1471 Edward IV defeated Queen Margaret of Anjou's Lancastrians at Tewkesbury in one of the bloodiest battles of the Wars of the Roses. Nibley Green, near Dursley, was the scene of the last pitched battle between private armies in England. This was in 1470, when William Berkeley's defeat of Lord Lisle settled the disputed inheritance of the Berkeley estates. The Berkeleys figure frequently in Gloucestershire's history.

There were several skirmishes during the Civil War. Berkeley Castle, for example, was a Royalist stronghold until captured after a three-day siege. However, the most dramatic event of that war in the county was the siege of Gloucester in August-September 1643, when the Parliamentary city held out successfully against the Royalists until relieved by a force which marched from London. The position of Gloucester endangered the route between the king's headquarters at Oxford and his loyal followers in South Wales, so this was a setback for the Royalists in a year in which they enjoyed many triumphs. Neither did it help the king that the Cotswold clothiers supported Parliament. Cromwell later commandeered the cloth of the Stroud valleys to put his New Model Army in uniforms.

The woollen trade made Gloucestershire rich. Cotswold wool had established a high reputation long before the fourteenth century when it was exported to Flanders and Italy. The wealthy merchants who traded the wool built fine houses and endowed their towns with the great 'wool churches'. Attention later turned to producing woollen cloth and water-powered mills were established, most notably in the Stroud district. Only in the early nineteenth century did the industry lose out to the rapidly rising textile district of West Yorkshire. This brought a severe depression, with a mass emigration of weavers from around Stroud to North America and Australia in 1837. Within a few years related industries were developed, such as making carpets, fibreboards and chemical dyes. Silk was important for a time until that too declined.

The Forest of Dean was an important industrial area, where the timber was used for charcoal burning or shipbuilding and there were iron and coal mines and iron foundries. Redbrook on the Wye had copper and tin plate works. Sandstone is still quarried in the Forest of Dean, but the Cotswold limestone is world-famous as a building material, seen in the villages and towns which are so much enjoyed by tourists. Other Gloucestershire industries include ironfounding, matchmaking, pin-making and carriage building at Gloucester. In the modern age the wide Severn estuary was chosen to provide cooling water for nu-

The river Severn at Ashleworth.

clear power stations at Berkeley and Oldbury, the former already at the end of its working life and the latter now in Avon.

Farming is a traditional occupation but, while sheep still graze the steeper slopes, the Cotswolds are now important for arable farming too. Dairying developed in the vales and the county is famed for its Double Gloucester cheese, which was first developed from the milk of the Old Gloucester breed of cattle. Fruit is grown in the vales, such as apples, with their attendant cidermaking industry, and plums. The salmon and eel fisheries on the Severn river are other activities of long standing.

As in any county, good communications have always been important. The Roman road system is still recognisable in the Cotswolds, where Cirencester remains a route centre. The Fosse Way is followed for a long way by the A429, and Ermine Way is taken by the A417 north-west to Gloucester and the A419 south-east to Swindon. The old Roman road between Gloucester and Bristol became the A38, a road which was once the bane of motorists but is now largely superseded by the M5 motorway.

The river Severn was a great natural water-way into the Midlands. Thus the estuary was an important outlet for the trade of this large hinterland and inevitably Gloucester became an entrepot with riverside quays. After 1827 the Gloucester and Sharpness Canal brought ships to the new docks in the heart of the city. The Wye was also a waterway, being tidal as far as Bigsweir Bridge and navigable to Redbrook and beyond. Sharpness is now the only port in the county, but places such as Lydney once shipped coal from the Forest of Dean, and there were numerous small quays and shipping places, as at Berkeley Pill or Newnham. Of Gloucestershire's canals, the Stroudwater and the Thames and Severn Canals linked the two main navigable river systems, opening up a new cross-country route for trade with London.

Railways transformed the county's communications. Although built independently, many were taken over by the Great Western and Midlands Railways. The first railways were short horse-worked tramroads built in the early nineteenth century to serve the coal mines in the Forest of Dean. The first main-line system in Gloucestershire was the Birmingham and Gloucester Railway, which reached Cheltenham and Gloucester in 1840.

The route was continued by the Bristol and Gloucester Railway in 1844, but this broad-gauge line necessitated an awkward transfer of traffic at Gloucester until both were taken over by the Midland Railway a few years later. The barrier of the Cotswold Hills was overcome by a tunnel at Sapperton when the Cheltenham and Great Western Union Railway was opened in 1847 to link London with Gloucester and Cheltenham via Stroud. On this line, the 'Cheltenham Flyer' was billed the fastest express in the world, although its record section was between Swindon and Paddington. The main line between Oxford and Evesham passes through the north-east corner of the county, via Moreton-in-Marsh and a tunnel near Chipping Campden. The old South Wales Railway is the main route from the Midlands, via Gloucester, Chepstow and Newport. It is also an insurance for Paddington traffic against closure of the Severn Tunnel. Before the 1960s there was a complex of routes in and around the Cotswolds. Closed lines include the Banbury and Cheltenham Railway (1887-1962), which took in Stow-on-the-Wold, Bourton-on-the-Water and Andoversford, but Cirencester, Lechlade, Dursley, Nailsworth and Tetbury were all served by other lines.

FAMOUS PEOPLE

One of the earliest well known men associated with Gloucestershire was Richard (Dick) Whittington, who was born at Pauntley in about 1358. The Indian administrator Warren Hastings (1732-1818), although born in Oxfordshire, was buried at Daylesford church close to his ancestral seat just east of Stow-on-the-Wold. In contrast, one of England's greatest sportsmen, the cricketer W. G. Grace (1848-1915), was born at Downend near Bristol, then in Gloucestershire. The Gloucestershire Cricket Club for which he played is still based in Bristol, although matches are also held at Cheltenham College and Gloucester.

There were religious men too, such as William Tyndale, who translated and printed the Bible in English and was martyred in 1536. He was born near North Nibley, where he is remembered by a tall monument at Nibley Knoll. John Hooper, the extreme Protestant Bishop of Gloucester, was also martyred for his beliefs in 1555. The evangelist George Whitefield was born in 1714 at the Bell Inn, Gloucester. The foundation of the Sunday school movement in 1780 is attributed to an-

The monument to John Hooper, Gloucester's martyred bishop.

other Gloucester man, Robert Raikes, although William King of Dursley may have been earlier. Fairford was the birthplace of John Keble (1792-1866), who revived the Church of England and has an Oxford college named after him.

In the world of science and pioneers, the astronomer James Bradley was born at Sherborne in 1693. He succeeded Halley as Astronomer-Royal in 1742, died twenty years later at Chalford and was buried at Minchinhampton. Jonathon Hulls of Chipping Campden patented a steam tug in 1738, although it failed its trials on the Avon at Evesham. Sir George Onesiphorus Paul was a pioneer of prison reform which included security, health and the separation of prisoners according to age and sex. His new 'houses of correction', designed by William Blackburn in 1790, were at Gloucester, Littledean, Northleach and Bristol. Dr Edward Jenner (1749-1823), proclaimed as the inventor of the smallpox vaccination, was born and practised at Berkeley. He went to school at Wotton-under-Edge, the town where Isaac Pitman invented his system of shorthand writing in

1837. Robert Forester Mushet (1811-91), who was born at Coleford in the Forest of Dean, was at the forefront of steelmaking technology. He contributed to Bessemer's process and improved upon the cutting speeds of tool steel by the addition of alloys. Dr Edward Wilson, the Antarctic explorer and one of Captain Scott's ill-fated companions, was born in Cheltenham in 1872.

Gloucestershire has had its share of prominent names in the arts. The composer Gustav Holst was born in 1874 at Cheltenham, where there is now a museum in his honour. Another famous composer, Ralph Vaughan Williams, was born in 1872 at Down Ampney, the village which gives its name to the tune of the hymn 'Come down, O love divine'. Ivor Gurney (1890-1937), the First World War poet and composer, was born in Gloucester. The writer Laurie Lee told of his childhood at Slad near Stroud in his famed book *Cider with Rosie*. Another Cotswold childhood is described in Nancy Mitford's *The Pursuit of Love*. The craftsman and poet William Morris (1834-96) lived just to the east of Lechlade at Kelmscot in Oxfordshire. He was a founder of the Arts and Crafts Movement, believing that craftsmen should take a pride in skilled and worthwhile jobs in pleasant surroundings. Several followers of the movement became associated with the Cotswolds, among them Ernest Gimson and the brothers Ernest and Sydney Barnsley, who set up workshops at Sapperton around 1900.

Today, the county has royal residents: the Prince and Princess of Wales at Highgrove House near Tetbury, and the Princess Royal at Gatcombe Park near Minchinhampton.

THE COTSWOLDS

The famous Cotswold Hills are an Area of Outstanding Natural Beauty, aligned southwest to north-east across the eastern half of Gloucestershire, but extending a little outside the county. The underlying Jurassic limestones have given the area its most characteristic features. The Cotswolds plateau dips gently eastwards into Oxfordshire, its hills ranging from 400 feet (122 metres) to around 800-900 feet (244-74 metres). This plateau surface made possible the construction of a great number of wartime airfields, many of which can still be traced. The Cotswolds reach 1083 feet (330 metres) at Cleeve Common. There are superb viewpoints from this high ground along the western edge, which is bounded by a dramatic scarp slope descending to the Severn Vale. This distinct Cotswold

The Slad valley, the setting for Laurie Lee's 'Cider with Rosie'.

Edge, often clothed in beech woods, is heavily dissected by valleys around Stroud and Dursley. Stinchcombe Hill is almost an outlier, just joined by a narrow ridge between the Dursley valley and Waterley Bottom. True outliers of the Cotswolds are the isolated Robinswood Hill and Churchdown at Gloucester. Alderton Hill is another, dwarfed by the massive bulk of Bredon Hill across in Hereford and Worcester.

The Thames has its source near Cirencester and most other rivers flow south-east into it, namely the Churn, Coln, Leach, Windrush and Evenlode. The main exception is the Frome, which follows the general trend before swinging westwards at Sapperton, passing through the deep Golden Valley to Stroud and the Severn at Framilode. The Thames and Severn Canal made use of this valley before tunnelling under the hills at Sapperton. Elsewhere, the Isbourne flows north at Winchcombe to meet the Warwickshire Avon at Evesham.

The Cotswold stone, with mellow colours ranging from a pale buff to browns and yellows, and its almost exclusive use as a building material, has made the architecture of the Cotswold villages and towns more 'English' than any other area in the country. The delightful houses and perfect English village

Dry-stone walling in the Cotswolds.

scenes are justly popular and sought by tourists. Traditionally, the freestones were dressed for masonry, and the thinner beds were split for roofing 'slates'. Less prized stones were extensively used for dry-stone walling, which affects the wider rural landscape. Old quarries pit the landscape near many villages and along the Cotswold Edge.

Sheep farming brought riches in the middle ages and the earlier centres, with fine churches endowed by rich wool merchants, were Chipping Campden, Cirencester, Fairford and Northleach. Cotswold wool was famous throughout Europe. During the seventeenth century the emphasis changed from wool to the production of higher-valued finished woollen cloth and with it new centres developed where there was a supply of water for washing, dyeing and fulling. The water became a source of power when the cottage industry transferred to large-scale production in mills. This movement was to the south and west, particularly at Stroud and Dursley but also at Bisley, Minchinhampton, Nailsworth, Painswick and Tetbury.

Cirencester is the true 'capital' of the Cotswolds, with other popular centres along the old Fosse Way at Bourton-on-the-Water, Stow-on-the-Wold and Moreton-in-Marsh. Chipping Campden, Painswick, Tetbury, Winchcombe and Wotton-under-Edge are all of interest, the last two beneath the high Cotswolds. Stroud is the largest town, developed as a textile-manufacturing centre in a deep valley. Bibury, the Slaughters and the Swells are well known, but there are many other small villages and hamlets which are just as attractive and all worth exploring in the Cotswolds' quiet valleys. A different aspect of rural settlement was the establishment of anti-industrialist colonies in the nineteenth century, in an attempt to live off the land while rejecting the rising dependence of workers on industry in the cities. The Whiteway Colony, 5 miles (8 km) north-east of Stroud, was established in the 1890s by a group of Londoners, and some of the original timber houses remain.

THE SEVERN VALE

This is the broad lower Severn valley, with fertile lowlands beside the river liable to flooding. Some land is gently undulating, with one ridge of blue lias limestone rising to around 200 feet (60 metres). There are underlying marls and clays, which have been used for bricks and tiles for the houses in the vale's

Fairford church owes its fine architecture to the Cotswold wool trade.

scattered villages. The Vale of Gloucester is mainly to the north of the city of Gloucester, while the Vale of Berkeley is to the south. This is much narrower, being confined by the Cotswold scarp and the broadening Severn estuary. The west bank of the estuary is closely bounded by the Forest of Dean but Gloucestershire extends further downstream on this side, to include the Beachley peninsula. The river Leadon is a tributary of the Severn in the northwest corner of Gloucestershire, where the peaceful Vale of Leadon has orchards, market gardens, vineyards and attractive villages, with the main centre at Newent.

The Severn dominates the area and makes a great meander around the Arlingham peninsula, with further meanders at Framilode. The Bristol Channel and Severn estuary experience one of the greatest tidal ranges in the world, and it is the funnelling of the estuary here which causes the famous tidal bore, which can be up to 9 feet (2.7 metres) high. It can be seen from vantage points along the riverbank, such as at Minsterworth and Elmore. The local press gives a timetable of predicted bores. At low tide the tidal estuary has extensive mud and sand flats, but these can be very dangerous to the unwary as the tide rises at an alarming speed.

The Severn has always been a barrier. There are old fording and ferry points, for example between Purton West and East or Arlingham and Newnham. For centuries the lowest bridging point was at Gloucester, until the Severn Bridge was completed from Aust to Beachley in 1966. Since 1974 only the west end of the bridge on the Beachley peninsula stands in Gloucestershire, so that with the Wye Bridge this M4 crossing has the novelty of passing through three counties. Rail crossings of the estuary were earlier. The lowest in its day was the multi-span bridge of the Severn Bridge Railway, built in 1879 near Sharpness. After being damaged by a passing ship, it was demolished in 1969. Further downstream, the Severn Tunnel of 1886 is still a vital short cut from London to Wales, leaving the Gloucestershire (now Avon) shore at Pilning.

Severn trows were the sailing barges which passed upstream from Bristol to the tidal limit at Gloucester, and beyond to Worcester and Stourport. Smaller vessels could reach Ironbridge, Shrewsbury and even Welshpool. Commercial traffic on this waterway continued into the twentieth century but has now ceased. The meandering Severn estuary was avoided by the Gloucester and Sharpness Canal of 1827, England's second largest ship canal and still used by pleasure craft. There is still a flourishing trade at Sharpness docks.

FOREST OF DEAN

The Royal Forest of Dean is indeed a contrast with the rest of Gloucestershire. This area of oak forest, a royal hunting ground of kings since 1016, lies in the triangle between the Severn estuary and lower Wye. It was designated the first National Forest Park in England in 1938, and much is administered by the Forestry Commission from its headquarters at Coleford. Today conifers are grown in plantations too. There is a Scenic Drive of 14 miles (22 km), but away from the roads there are footpaths throughout the forest where visitors can enjoy the scenery or explore the natural history or industrial heritage. Around the fringes are longer paths, such as the Offa's Dyke Path and Wye Valley Walk along the Welsh border. The Forest's wildlife includes fallow deer, pied flycatchers in the Nag's Head nature reserve and peregrine falcons at the famous viewpoint of Symonds Yat Rock.

Dean has a varied geology of Carboniferous age, with limestone, sandstone and exposed coal measures all influencing man's activities. After hunting, the forest was a great supplier of timber for the navy, with ships built at Lydney. Nelson came here in 1803 to advise on the replanting and management of oaks to ensure a supply of timber for shipbuilding, for stocks had become depleted by charcoal burning. The charcoal burners supplied the Forest's iron industry. Iron has been mined since the iron age and Roman times, and the now overgrown pits and mounds are known as 'scowles', as at Bream's Eaves, Devil's Chapel and Puzzle Wood. Underground workings can be explored at Clearwell Caves. Associated with iron mining was the smelting and working of the metal into various products including wire, pins and nails, as in the Soudley valley. At Coleford Robert Mushet developed the Bessemer process in the mid nineteenth century and made further improvements in the production of steel. The seams of the Forest of Dean's coalfield were faulted and difficult to work and the last colliery was closed in 1965. Today 'Freeminers' work small drift mines (gales) for coal in the forest. The Court of Verderers still meets at Speech House in the heart of the forest to uphold the ancient customs and privileges of the inhabitants. There are rights of grazing, and mining laws for the Freeminers, who were granted this privilege by Edward I. A network of railways served the iron and coal industries and their courses can be followed through the forest. The Dean Forest Railway follows a restored section of track near Lydney, a Severnside coal port with a canal and lock gates.

Coleford is considered the 'capital' of Dean, while derelict coal mines around Cinderford are evidence of its development as a coal-mining town. On a much smaller scale, Parkend is a colliery village in the Cannop valley. In contrast, around the forest edge are St Briavels Castle and Lydney Park, with gardens and a Roman temple site. The Dean Heritage Centre at Soudley gives an excellent overall view of the history of the area.

'Freeminers' in 1974, pushing a coal truck out of a drift mine.

Springtime in the Cannop Valley, Forest of Dean.

2
Countryside

Blaize Bailey, near Littledean, Forest of Dean. 1 mile (1.6 km) south of Littledean.

This viewpoint and picnic area on the forest edge commands good views over the Newnham bend of the Severn and the vale beyond. There is also a forest trail.

Cannop Valley, near Parkend, Forest of Dean.

The B4234 follows the Cannop Valley for 4 miles (6 km) north from Parkend and gives easy access to several picnic areas and forest trails, most notably at Cannop Ponds. It is also accessible from the B4226.

Cleeve Common and Cleeve Hill, Southam, near Cheltenham. Easily accessible from the B4632 (formerly A46), near Southam, 3 miles (5 km) north-east of Cheltenham.

The vista from this high viewpoint on the Cotswold scarp encompasses much of the Severn Vale, from which stand out the towers of Gloucester Cathedral and Tewkesbury Ab-

bey. Beyond can be seen the whole length of the Malvern Hills, May Hill and the Black Mountains. There is disturbance from quarrying all along the edge of Cleeve Cloud, but the grassland above covers 3 square miles (8 sq km) and is the largest area of common on the Cotswolds, which rise to their highest point, at 1083 feet (330 metres), above Prestbury.

Coaley Peak Picnic Site, near Nympsfield. Beside the B4066 halfway between Dursley and Stroud.

There are good views out over the Vale of Berkeley, across the upper Severn estuary to the Forest of Dean and Welsh mountains on the far side. This very accessible site has a picnic area and nature trails among the wooded slopes of Frocester Hill below. The Cotswold Way passes along the edge here. The Nympsfield chambered tomb can also be seen (chapter 3).

11

On Cleeve Hill.

Cooper's Hill, near Brockworth.

The hill is reached from the A46, as it climbs the wooded Cotswold edge to the south-east of Gloucester. An exciting event is held here every May on Spring Bank Holiday Monday, when there are races for competitors who chase wildly down a 1 in 2 slope after rolling Double Gloucester cheeses. This annual tradition dates back to at least the fifteenth century but is probably much earlier. It is said to maintain grazing rights on the hill. For the less energetic, there is a nature reserve here, with trails in Brockworth Wood. Higher up alongside the A46 there is a picnic area and viewpoint overlooking Gloucester and its vale.

Cotswold Way, Chipping Campden to Alderley.

This long-distance footpath of 97 miles (155 km) runs from Chipping Campden to Bath. Most is in Gloucestershire, where it passes along the high Cotswolds via beauty spots, viewpoints, woodlands and villages. It has been clearly waymarked by the volunteer Cotswold Wardens and the Gloucestershire Ramblers' Association. A small portion enters Hereford and Worcester at Broadway and the path leaves the county altogether at Alderley near Wotton-under-Edge to continue south through Avon to Bath.

Crickley Hill Country Park, near Birdlip. Telephone: 0452 863170 or 425675. Gloucestershire County Council and National Trust.

This important promontory with an iron age hillfort and earlier neolithic site (chapter 3) is a Site of Special Scientific Interest and has a visitor centre, waymarked nature trails and the geology exposed in a quarry on the escarpment. The view is magnificent.

Dover's Hill, 1 mile (1.6 km) north-west of Chipping Campden. National Trust.

The first viewpoint on the Cotswold Way, with a wide view over the Vale of Evesham, Dover's Hill is reached from a lane between Chipping Campden and Weston-sub-Edge. It is a great natural bowl or amphitheatre on the Cotswold edge. Robert Dover's Games, or the 'Cotswold Games', took place here from 1610 until 1852. Now revived, they are held here on the Friday after the Spring Bank Holiday. The curious holed Kiftsgate Stone stood on Dover's Hill until 1878 but can now be found with difficulty beside a lane just to the south-west.

Forest of Dean

The surviving 40 square miles (102 sq km) of forest have been administered by the Forestry Commission since 1924. Although there are more recent plantations of conifers, there are ancient oaks and many woodlands which were planted during the Napoleonic Wars. The forest edges are an attractive combination of forest and pasture enclosed by tree-lined hedges. Of added interest, there are many overgrown traces of coal and iron mines, quarries and railways (chapter 7). Throughout the forest, the Commission provides marked trails, picnic sites and camp sites. There is a sculpture trail from the Beechenhurst picnic site. Some of the beauty spots are included in this chapter, but for more information contact the Forestry Commission, Crown Office, Bank Street, Coleford, Gloucestershire GL16 8BA. Telephone: 0594 33057.

Haresfield Beacon, 3 miles (5 km) north-west of Stroud. National Trust.

At 713 feet (217 metres), this promontory of the Cotswold scarp has superb views across the Severn Vale as far as the Brecon Beacons and, it is said, down to Exmoor. The spur was the ideal site for a fortification in the iron age (see chapter 3). The steep slopes of Standish Wood and Randwick Wood to the south and Scottsquar Hill to the east are also National Trust properties.

Highnam Woods Nature Reserve, near Highnam. On the north side of the A40, 3^1/$_2$ miles (6 km) west of Gloucester.

This ancient woodland overlooking the Severn Vale was purchased in 1987 by the Royal Society for the Protection of Birds to safeguard its large population of nightingales.

Kilkenny Viewpoint, near Andoversford.

There is access for cars from the A436 to this viewpoint which gives superb wide vistas across the Cotswolds, the Cotswold edge to Cleeve Common and northwards across the Severn Vale to the Malvern Hills and beyond.

Leckhampton Hill, Leckhampton, Cheltenham.

The Cotswold Way passes along the edge here, from which there are extensive views over Cheltenham and the vale beyond. The much repaired Devil's Chimney just below the escarpment is a pinnacle left behind by extensive quarrying in the late eighteenth century but is said to rise from hell. The stone was for Cheltenham, but the quarries are now mostly overgrown (chapter 7).

May Hill, north of the A40, 3 miles (5 km) south-west of Newent. National Trust.

At 971 feet (296 metres), this high hill provides views over the Forest of Dean to Wales. The summit (not National Trust) was planted with pines in 1887 for Queen Victoria's Golden Jubilee and more recently in 1977 and 1980 for the Queen's Silver Jubilee and the Queen Mother's eightieth birthday. The domed hill, with its conspicuous summit

trees, is readily recognised from many viewpoints in the Severn Vale and along the Cotswold edge.

Minchinhampton Common, near Minchinhampton. National Trust.

The common is a high and airy plateau with open views over the Stroud and Nailsworth valleys on either side. Part is used as a golf course. Ancient earthworks such as the Bulwarks and Amberley Camp are described in chapter 3. The whole is surrounded by the villages of Amberley, Box, Burleigh and Minchinhampton (chapter 9). The smaller Rodborough Common is a little to the north.

Nagshead Nature Reserve, near Parkend, Forest of Dean. Off the B4431, just west of Parkend.

The Royal Society for the Protection of Birds manages this 760 acre (308 ha) woodland of oak, beech and other hardwoods. Over three hundred nestboxes provide homes for pied flycatchers, but woodpeckers, nuthatches and tree-creepers can also be seen. There are footpaths and marked trails, and an information centre is open during the summer.

New Fancy View, near Parkend, Forest of Dean. Just off the B4431 about one mile (1.6 km) north-east of Parkend.

Here are a picnic area, forest trail and high

The Devil's Chimney, Leckhampton Hill.

viewpoint on the well landscaped waste tip of a coal mine. Down the road to the east there is a lakeside picnic area at Mallards Pike.

Offa's Dyke Path, Sedbury Cliffs to Redbrook.

This long-distance footpath along the Welsh border was opened in 1971. Of its 170 miles (272 km), a very attractive section of 14 miles (22 km) is in Gloucestershire, starting or ending on the shore of the Severn estuary at Sedbury Cliffs (near Chepstow) and following the late eighth-century earthwork (chapter 3) as closely as possible on the mainly wooded east side of the Wye valley as far as Redbrook. There are good glimpses of the Wye valley through the trees, especially from the Devil's Pulpit, which looks down on the ruins of Tintern Abbey, far below on the other bank of the river in Gwent.

Robinswood Hill Country Park, Reservoir Road, Gloucester. Telephone: 0452 413029.

On the very edge of Gloucester, the hill is an outlier of the main Cotswolds, which lie to the east. The large country park has a visitor centre (from which guided walks can be arranged) and extensive nature trails and horse trails. On the west side, an old quarry is a Site of Special Scientific Interest because it contains the best inland exposure of Lower and Middle Lias rocks in England. The hill is 651 feet (198 metres) high and a topograph at the summit explains the extensive view over the lower Severn valley and five counties. There are also a BMX track and dry ski slope here (see chapter 8).

Seven Springs, near Coberley, 3 miles (5 km) south of Cheltenham.

Steps lead down to seven springs emerging from the foot of a dry-stone wall, next to a lay-by across the A436 from the Seven Springs Inn. This is said to be the highest source of the Thames in the sense of its tributary the river Churn, high up almost at the crest of the Cotswold scarp. It is far more interesting than the true source of the Thames at Trewsbury Mead, where the spring is intermittent and dries up in summer months. This is at Thameshead, 3 miles (5 km) south-west of Cirencester.

Soudley Ponds and Sutton Bottom, Upper Soudley, Forest of Dean.

Trees surround an attractive pond in a tributary valley across the B4227 from the Dean Heritage Centre (chapter 7). There is a forest trail in Foundry Wood and there is a walk up the valley to further ponds at Sutton Bottom. This latter can be reached by car along the lane from Upper Soudley to Littledean, and the viewpoint at Blaize Bailey (see above) is also nearby.

Speech House Woodland, Forest of Dean. On the B4226, just north-east of the Speech House Hotel.

Here there is a picnic place with forest trails in oak woodland. There is also an arboretum. The Verderers' Court still meets at the Speech House to maintain the ancient laws of the forest.

Symonds Yat Rock, Forest of Dean. 3½ miles (6 km) north of Coleford on the B4432.

This famous viewpoint is right on the county border, so that the visitor stands in Gloucestershire but admires the sweep of the Wye and the picturesque scenery of Hereford and Worcester. Rare peregrine falcons are an additional attraction. Since 1982 the Royal Society for the Protection of Birds and the Forestry Commission have encouraged these birds of prey to nest and breed here after an absence of thirty years.

Tyndale Monument, Nibley Knoll, North Nibley. On the B4060 between Dursley and Wotton-under-Edge.

This prominent landmark is a monument to the locally born William Tyndale, who first translated and printed the Old and New Testaments in English but was martyred in Flanders in 1536. It is a stone tower 111 feet (34 metres) high. Its erection in 1886 was financed by a public subscription. There are fine views from here over the Vale of Berkeley.

Wintour's Leap, Broadrock.

This is a viewpoint above a 250 foot (76 metre) cliff overlooking the Lancaut bend in the tidal Wye river, 1½ miles (2 km) upstream from Chepstow. This very steep cliff of Carboniferous limestone has been quarried so it must be far more dramatic now than it was in 1642 when Sir John Wintour is said to have leapt over on his horse when pursued by the Parliamentarians. He survived and swam to safety before fleeing to France by ship from Chepstow. Despite a narrow access from the B4228 which passes very close to the cliff, it is worth finding the viewpoint.

3
Places of archaeological interest

There is evidence for man in Gloucestershire far back in prehistory, but the earliest monuments date from the time of the first farmers in the neolithic period, sometime after about 4000 BC. Many long barrows with chambered tombs survive down the length of the Cotswolds – one of England's special areas for such tombs. Their style, long trapezoidal mounds with an inturned forecourt, is matched by others west of the Severn into South Wales as far as the Gower peninsula. They belong to the Severn-Cotswold group which has affinities with similar tombs in Brittany, and they may represent the arrival of a people or religious idea via the Bristol Channel. As with other long barrows, these tombs were for collective burials. There are two types: those with a passage and side chambers opening from the wide end, and barrows with side chambers. Hetty Pegler's Tump near Dursley can be entered, as can small side chambers at the Belas Knap tomb near Winchcombe. The latter has a prominent false entrance, a feature found at other sites. The very low Hazleton

tomb (now destroyed) was excavated in 1979-82 under modern conditions, unlike so many other tombs which were opened in the nineteenth century when techniques were less sophisticated. The cairn was found to have been surrounded by a dry-stone wall and constructed with a series of internal walls to help retain its shape. Side chambers contained the bones of at least 23 individuals. Material for the cairn was dug from side ditches or quarries, in which were ritually placed red-deer antlers.

Neolithic religion was not just concerned with burying the dead. An important site was Crickley Hill, where excavators have found a causewayed enclosure which later became a defended settlement, perhaps a religious centre, protected by a fence and gateway. Concentrations of leaf-shaped flint arrowheads around the two entrances and signs of burning suggest the site was attacked and destroyed.

Many of the bronze age round barrows in the Cotswolds are tree-covered, such as Nan Tow's Tump, and it was not until the iron age

The Woodchester mosaic at the last uncovering in 1974.

that hillforts were constructed on spectacular spurs of the Cotswold scarp. Crickley Hill is one, twice the size of the neolithic enclosure which lay beneath, but there is a line of hillforts southwards from Nottingham Hill to Brackenbury Ditches, continuing to Old Sodbury (formerly in Gloucestershire). The people were the Dobunni, whose territory extended into Oxfordshire, Somerset and Wiltshire. Their tribal centre was at Bagendon near Cirencester. The lack of extensive 'Celtic' fields, such as are found in other regions such as the chalk downs of southern England, suggests that the Cotswolds were grazed by sheep and that wool was already important.

Gloucestershire is especially famous as a Roman county. By AD 47, the initial Roman frontier followed the Fosse Way. A fort was established near Gloucester at Kingsholm beside the lowest crossing on the Severn on the route into South Wales, to be replaced around AD 64-6 by a much larger fortress. In AD 97 the *colonia* of Gloucester (*Glevum*) was founded for veteran legionaries, who were a military reserve for emergencies. Bagendon was replaced by Cirencester (*Corinium Dobunnorum*) as the regional centre or *civitas*. The town grew to become the second largest in Roman Britain, no doubt enhanced by the riches brought by wool. The largest fourth-century mosaic workshop in Britain is believed to have been here, producing a style known as the *Corinium* school. Tewkesbury has traces of a Roman town which could be the lost *Argistillum* of the Ravenna Cosmography. There was a Roman settlement within the iron age site of Salmonsbury at Bourton-on-the-Water, where the Fosse Way crosses the Windrush river. Dorn, near Moreton-in-Marsh, was a small walled settlement of 10 acres (4 ha) on the west side of the Fosse Way. The largest agricultural settlement in the Cotswolds was at Kingscote, south-west of Cirencester. Cult sites with temples are exposed at Lydney Park and Littledean in the Forest of Dean.

Both *Glevum* and *Corinium* were surrounded by rich villas, such as Chedworth, Witcombe and Woodchester. The last site, now covered, was a very fine villa excavated by Samuel Lysons in 1793-6. It had over sixty rooms and a superb Orpheus mosaic made in about AD 325 by the *Corinium* school. At least five villas appear to have been attacked in AD 367. A villa at Frocester Court had a possible woolshed, as well as evidence for growing

St Mary's Priory, Deerhurst: the Saxon west wall of the nave.

wheat and barley, and so-called shears were found at Chedworth. The general lack of spindle whorls and loom weights suggests that most of the wool was exported from the region.

The best known Roman road in Gloucestershire is the Fosse Way, which follows the Cotswolds through the county. At *Corinium* it met the Ermine Way and Akeman Street. The lines of many others can be traced, but a section of road is preserved at Blackpool Bridge in the Forest of Dean. It was in this district that the Romans worked for iron, and their old workings are called scowles. They mined coal here too. The Cotswold stone was in great demand by the Romans, for walling, columns, roofing tiles, tombstones, shrines and other sculptures.

In post-Roman times, there are indications that parts of some villas continued to be occupied into the fifth century. The hillfort at Crickley Hill was re-occupied. Later Saxon evidence is seen in the stonework of a good number of the county's churches. Deerhurst is unique in having two Saxon-period churches.

16

Examples of Saxon carved stone crosses can be seen in Gloucester City Museum. The greatest earthwork of this period is Offa's Dyke, constructed in the late eighth century by Offa of Mercia against the Welsh. Although not complete throughout its whole length, there are good sections where it follows the Gloucestershire side of the Wye valley gorge.

The Corinium Museum at Cirencester is worth visiting for its Roman content alone. Museums at Gloucester and Cheltenham have important collections, but many local museums have archaeological material too. The name of each site is followed by the Ordnance Survey 1:50,000 map sheet on which it appears, together with the six-figure grid reference.

Bagendon Dykes, Bagendon (OS 163: SP 018064).

Overgrown linear earthworks can be seen alongside lanes just east of Bagendon village, 1 mile (1.6 km) south of North Cerney. They enclose the site of the late iron age *oppidum* or tribal centre of the Dobunni. There was a mint here. Finds are in the Corinium Museum at Cirencester (chapter 6).

Beckbury Camp, Hailes Abbey (OS 163: SP 064299).

This small iron age hillfort of about 4½ acres (1.8 ha) is situated on a promontory edge of the Cotswold scarp high above Hailes Abbey. The east and south are defended by a rampart and ditch with some evidence of construction with dry-stone walling.

Belas Knap long barrow, near Winchcombe (OS 163: SP 021254). English Heritage.

It is well worth the steep climb to visit this well known and unusual neolithic chambered cairn, which is 170 feet (51.8 metres) long and revetted with dry-stone walling. The north end turns inwards to form a forecourt with a false entrance behind which there is no chamber. However, four small chambers have been found in the sides and south end of the long cairn. Excavations in the mid nineteenth century and again in 1928-30 located the bones of thirty individuals in the chambers, and those of five children and a man's skull behind the false entrance. Some finds are in the Cheltenham Art Gallery and Museum and the Winchcombe Museum (chapter 6). The Cotswold Way passes the tomb.

Roman road at Blackpool Bridge, Forest of Dean.

Blackpool Bridge Roman road, Forest of Dean (OS 162: SO 653087).

This section of so-called Roman road is beside the lane to Upper Soudley from the B4431, and between an old railway bridge and river bridge. It is 8 feet (2.4 metres) wide, paved and edged with a kerb. It seems to ford the stream just upstream of Blackpool Bridge, a structure which may also contain Roman masonry in its lower courses. If this is a Roman road, it must be associated with the mining activities which are known to have taken place in the Forest of Dean.

Brackenbury Ditches, North Nibley (OS 162: ST 747949).

A rampart and ditch defend this small iron age promontory fort, with the weaker side protected by two banks and ditches. A hollow way on the south side leads to the entrance. The site is in woodland on the next spur south from Tyndale's Monument on Nibley Knoll (chapter 2).

Chedworth Roman villa, Yanworth, near Northleach (OS 163: SP 053134). Telephone: 024289 256. National Trust.

This large and well preserved villa was discovered by accident in 1864 and subsequently excavated. The site lies in a shel-

tered position in a side valley, surrounded by trees, and was occupied from about AD 120 until the late fourth century. 32 rooms of the main wings have been excavated and exposed and include mosaics, hypocausts and a bath-house. There is a visitor centre and small domestic finds are displayed in the site museum, which was erected in 1866.

Cirencester Roman town (OS 163: SP 027022 and 020013).

Corinium was the second largest town in Roman Britain, and the Corinium Museum in Park Street contains many excavated finds (chapter 6). A section of the Roman town defences (SP 027022) is preserved in the Abbey Grounds. A stone wall was erected in the late second century on an earlier earth rampart, with a ditch outside. Outlines show the position of bastions which were added to the wall in the early fourth century. Far more impressive is the second-century amphitheatre (SP 020013), which is accessible from Cotswold Avenue to the south of the ring road. It is an elliptical embankment of quarry waste obtained from the immediate area, the whole originally retained by a dry-stone wall. It replaced an earlier timber structure and could seat six thousand spectators.

The Roman amphitheatre at Cirencester.

Cleeve Hill Camp, Southam, near Cheltenham (OS 163: SO 985255).

This high hill above Cheltenham has several iron age earthworks, disturbed by past quarrying and a golf course. The double banks and ditches of a hillfort can be seen around the summit, while the small earthwork known as The Ring lies just to the north (SO 985266). An east-west cross-dyke across the ridge (SO 987263) may be a boundary between the territory of Cleeve Hill and the larger fort on Nottingham Hill.

Crickley Hill promontory fort, near Birdlip (OS 163: SO 928161). National Trust and Gloucestershire County Council.

Within the country park (chapter 2) are the low earthworks of a causewayed enclosure dating from around 3000 BC. It is a site of great significance. Long-term excavations have revealed that this settlement was defended, while signs of burning and many flint arrowheads point to a violent end. There is also a ritual long mound of the same period. The promontory was again occupied in the iron age after about 600 BC by a fort of 9 acres (3.6 ha). The positions of post-holes have been marked on the ground to show the outlines of early rectangular long houses and round houses of a later phase. The site was again occupied in the dark ages or post-Roman period. The Barrow Wake viewpoint off the A417 towards Birdlip gives a clear view of how the iron age rampart cuts off the promontory.

Gloucester Roman town (OS 162: SO 832183, 833184 and 833185).

Following the building of a large fortress of 43 acres (17.4 ha) in about AD 64-6, the *colonia* of Gloucester (*Glevum*) was established here in AD 97 for veteran legionaries. A *vicus* or settlement also grew around the fort. Substantial foundation stones of the third-century town wall of *Glevum* can be seen in three places. There is a good section exposed beneath the floor of the archaeological section of the City Museum and Art Gallery in Brunswick Road. Not far away, there are large Roman stones beneath the later medieval wall at the Eastgate (SO 833184), and there is further evidence at the King's Walk Bastion (SO 833185). All three sites are administered by the Gloucester Museum Service (see chapter 6).

Hetty Pegler's Tump.

Haresfield Beacon hillfort, Haresfield (OS 162: SO 823090). Part National Trust.

This spur of the Cotswold edge is a good viewpoint (chapter 2) and well suited for defence. It would seem that the end of the spur, which includes Ring Hill, was defended in the iron age by a single rampart and ditch. A later extension enclosed Haresfield Hill, on the east side of the lane across the hill.

Hetty Pegler's Tump or Uley Tumulus, near Uley (OS 162: SO 789000). English Heritage.

This is the best neolithic chambered tomb in the Cotswolds, reconstructed with dry-stone walls and a huge stone giving a height of only 2 feet 3 inches (0.7 metre) at the entrance. Of the two pairs of side chambers, only those on the south side are open. Excavations in 1821 and 1854 revealed several skeletons in the chambers, while outside the forecourt at the east end there were two skeletons and the teeth and jaws of wild boars. A Romano-British burial was inserted in the upper part of the long cairn, dated to around the time of Constantine by three coins. A torch is recommended when visiting this site, which is close to the B4066.

Lydney Park Roman temple.

Leckhampton Hill hillfort, Leckhampton (OS 163: SO 946183).

There is public access to Leckhampton Hill and the famous Devil's Chimney (chapters 2 and 7). The hillfort has a single rampart, which was faced with dry-stone walling and a ditch cut into the solid rock. It is a promontory fort, so the north and west sides look over what is now a quarry face. The east entrance had guard chambers.

Longstone, near Staunton, Forest of Dean (OS 162: SO 560121).

A leaning menhir of Pennant sandstone, 8 feet (2.4 metres) tall, the Longstone stands at the forest edge on the A4136 south-east of Staunton and near the junction with the B4431 to Coleford.

Lydney Park hillfort and Roman temple, Lydney (OS 162: SO 616027). Access on application to estate office.

This important site within sight of the Severn estuary, and in the most attractive setting of Lydney Park (see chapter 5), was excavated by Mortimer Wheeler in 1928-9. The ramparts of a late iron age fort set on a steep-sided spur between two valleys enclose an area occupied during the Roman period. The site appears to have become a pagan ritual centre just after AD 364, when Christianity was already established in the Roman world. Visitors can see the foundations of a temple of Nodens, associated with a healing cult. Nearby, a bath-house is perched at the top of a steep slope. Water was supplied from a large tank. Traces of a long building range and a large guest-house complex have been excavated but are no longer exposed. Excavated finds, including statuettes, the Lydney dog and a famous curse, are displayed in the Lydney Park Museum (chapter 6). There is also evidence that the Romans mined iron ore at two sites on the hill, with one small gallery showing pick marks on the walls.

Minchinhampton Common earthworks, near Minchinhampton (OS 162). National Trust.

There are numerous earthworks, some very large, on the high plateau top of Minchinhampton Common (see chapter 2). They are best seen from the air, but they can be traced on the ground. The largest is The Bulwarks, a curving earthwork on the south-east side (SO 857004 to 869012). It may be an iron age territorial boundary marker for enclosing stock rather than a defensive work, but excavation has shown that the ditch is cut into the rock, with the excavated stone being used to face the outer part of the bank. Pinfarthing Camp (SO 856003 to 852008) and Amberley Camp (SO 852009 to 851016) are two lesser, curving earthworks on the west side of the Common. They are believed to be much more recent than the iron age and not camps. However, the Cross-dyke (SO 842012 to 853014) is contemporary with The Bulwarks and it adjoins the Amberley Camp at right angles. Other earthworks on the Common include Whitfield's Tump (SO 854017), the remains of a neolithic long barrow so-called because the evangelist George Whitefield preached here.

Nan Tow's Tump, near Leighterton (OS 162: ST 803893).

Opposite a lane to Hillesley on the A46, 1¹/₂ miles (2 km) south-west of Leighterton, this large bronze age round barrow is 9 feet (2.7 metres) high, but rather obscured by trees. It is a local tradition that the witch Nan Tow was buried upright within the barrow.

Notgrove long cairn, near Notgrove (OS 163: SP 095212). English Heritage.

The ruins of a neolithic long cairn stand beside the A436, 1 mile (1.6 km) north-west of Notgrove. It was excavated in 1881 and the 1930s. There were two pairs of side chambers with a fifth chamber at the end of the gallery passage. Signs of burning, the skeletons of two individuals and animal bones were evi-

dence for rituals in the forecourt area. An earlier chamber within a circular cairn was found beneath the long cairn. This contained the crouched skeleton of a man of about 55, and on top of the domed roof was the skeleton of a young woman.

Nottingham Hill hillfort, Cleeve Hill (OS 163: SO 984284).

A huge area of 120 acres (48.6 ha) is enclosed by this iron age promontory fort. The greatest defence, up to 10 feet (3 metres) high, is across the south-east side, while the rest uses the natural defence of the steep scarp slope of the Cotswold edge. A hoard of late bronze age metalwork, including three swords, is displayed at the Cheltenham Art Gallery and Museum (chapter 6). The hill commands extensive views, being at 915 feet (279 metres) above sea-level. It can be seen from Cleeve Common (chapter 2) and Cleeve Hill Camp.

Nympsfield long cairn, near Nympsfield (OS 162: SO 794013). At the Coaley Peak picnic site (chapter 2).

The tomb is displayed in plan, with no roofing capstones. The two side chambers and

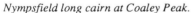

Nympsfield long cairn at Coaley Peak.

one end chamber were found to contain up to thirty skeletons. Nearby, but just outside the picnic area, is the round cairn known as the Soldier's Grave (SO 794015). This covered a boat-shaped pit containing many human and animal bones as well as late neolithic pottery.

Offa's Dyke earthwork, Sedbury Cliffs to Redbrook (OS 162: ST 552929 to SO 539091).

King Offa of Mercia built this major earthwork in AD 778-96 to define the western border of his kingdom with Wales. Some sections were never completed, but one of the better lengths is found along the extreme southwest border of Gloucestershire, where it makes use of the natural feature of the steep-sided Wye valley. The bank and ditch survive for much of this distance between Sedbury and Highbury Farm at Redbrook and can be seen by following the Offa's Dyke Path (see chapter 2). The best short section is for 2^1/$_2$ miles (4 km) through the woods from Tidenham (ST 551984) to Brockweir (SO 546011).

Painswick Beacon hillfort, near Painswick (OS 162: SO 869121).

The hill has commanding views and lies 1^1/$_2$ miles (2 km) north of Painswick, off the B4073 Gloucester road. The iron age hillfort on the summit has two ramparts and ditches and an inturned entrance on the east side. Quarrying has destroyed the interior, but a depression in the centre may be a ritual shaft. The fort has not been excavated.

Uley Bury hillfort, Uley (OS 162: ST 785990).

This is a classic site for a hillfort, with a flat hilltop and most sides surrounded by steep slopes. The interior of the 32 acre (13 ha) fort is not open, but footpaths from the B4066 at Uley follow the defences, which are almost rectangular in plan. They have been disturbed by quarrying, but it would appear that the main entrance was at the north corner. The fort was occupied in the iron age by the Dobunni; one of their coins, a copied gold stater, is in the museum at Stroud (chapter 6). Scattered finds of flints indicate that the hill may have been occupied as early as the neolithic period.

Welshbury Camp hillfort, near Cinderford (OS 162: SO 677155).

This hillfort, presumably of the iron age, lies 1^1/$_2$ miles (2 km) north-east of Cinderford. Access is by footpath through Welshbury Wood, which makes this unexcavated Forest of Dean site worth exploring. The gentler south and west sides are defended by a triple rampart. The entrance is in the south-east corner.

Witcombe Roman villa, Great Witcombe (OS 163: SO 899142). English Heritage.

The site is at the end of a long open lane signposted from the A417, tucked in a bowl under the Cotswold scarp just below Cooper's Hill Farm, with a vista across the Great Witcombe reservoirs to Crickley Hill (see above). The villa was excavated by Samuel Lysons after being discovered in 1818, with more recent work taking place in the 1930s and 1970s. The foundations exposed on this sloping site date from the mid third century, although the site was occupied at least two hundred years before. Two buildings now protect parts of the south-west wing, which includes a bath-house, latrines and mosaics.

Odda's Chapel (on the left) is one of two Saxon churches at Deerhurst, situated only two hundred yards apart.

4
Churches

Gloucestershire is noted for its churches, many with evidence of Saxon and Norman stonework. All have something of interest, from the humblest village church to the Cotswold wool churches and the great cathedral of Gloucester. A selection of the best examples is given here, while some town churches are described in chapter 9. Of other religious foundations, the ruins of Hailes Abbey, Kingswood Abbey and Llanthony Priory can be found in chapter 5.

Baunton: St Mary Magdalene.

This Norman church is in a tranquil part of the Churn valley. The main feature is a brightly coloured wall painting of St Christopher of the fourteenth century. A fifteenth-century embroidered altar cloth is also displayed.

Chedworth: St Andrew.

There is Norman work here, seen in the tower with its thirteenth-century belfry, and the arcade and north aisle of the tall fifteenth-century nave. The great windows of the nave give light to the interior where the stone wineglass-style pulpit and Norman font are of note. Outside, there are gargoyles and grotesques. The church and village are set at the head of a steep-sided valley, just over the hill from the Roman villa (chapter 3), although further around by road.

Chipping Campden: St James.

This is one of the great Cotswold wool churches, said to have been financed in part by William Grevel, who died in 1401. Some Norman and thirteenth-century work survives, but most is of a later date. The noble west tower is 120 feet (36 metres) high and dates from around 1490-1500. The tall nave of the same date has arcades supported by octagonal columns with concave sides identical to those at Northleach church. Other similarities are the clerestory windows and the great window over the chancel arch. Of the monuments, William Grevel's brass is set next to his wife Marion's in the chancel floor and is the largest in the county. In the sanctuary is the stone tomb of Thomas Smythe (died 1593), with his armoured figure reclining beneath a canopy and his two wives and thirteen children carved on the panels below. The South or Gainsborough Chapel contains the seventeenth-century black and white marble tomb of Sir Baptist Hicks and his wife, their effigies lying under a massive canopy. Their daughter Juliana and her husband, Edward Noel, are shown standing inside the open doors of another monument. The church has a cope of about 1400 and a unique pair of altar hangings of about 1500. Above the fourteenth-century porch is the muniment room, which contains displays relating to the church, charities and town.

Cirencester: St John the Baptist.

The church tower dominates the town and has curious buttresses rising from the end of the nave. The large south porch is also prominent and has two storeys above its fan-vaulted ceiling. It is almost detached from the main body of the church. Inside this wool church, the tall nave is striking, with a clerestory and window over the chancel arch as seen at Chipping Campden and Northleach. On the south side a wooden screen encloses the chapel and tomb of Henry Garstang, dating from the 1460s. The chancel is bounded by three chapels, of which the narrow Catherine Chapel has a fan-vaulted ceiling brought from Cirencester Abbey and fragments of wall paintings of St Nicholas. Next to it, the Lady Chapel contains the fine tomb and figures in period costume of Humphrey Bridges (died 1598) and his wife Elizabeth (died 1620) with their sons and daughters kneeling beneath. Both were generous to the poor, she giving six houses for six poor widows with six shillings for ever. Fifteenth and sixteenth-century brasses here and in the Trinity Chapel include Reginald Spicer and his four wives. One of the church's treasures is the Anne Boleyn Cup, displayed in a safe on the south side of the chancel arch. It is a silver gilded cup of 1535-6 and was given in 1563 by Dr Richard Master, physician to Elizabeth I.

Coberley: St Giles.

The church is approached through a door and private grounds. The sanctuary contains the only example of a heart burial in the Cotswolds, believed to be of Sir Giles de Berkeley, whose body was buried where he died at Malvern in 1295. The south chapel has the tomb and effigy of Sir Thomas Berkeley, who died in about 1350. He fought at Crécy and rebuilt the church just before his death. Next to him lies Lady Joan, who later married Sir William Whittington and was the mother of Sir Richard (Dick) Whittington. There are also two unnamed effigies of a small child and a young man. The south chapel and tower escaped a rebuilding by the Victorians. An arch in the churchyard wall opens on to the site

St Mary's Priory, Deerhurst: one of the animal-headed label stops.

of Coberley Hall, built in the fourteenth century by the Berkeleys and later the home of the Brydges, Chandos and Castleman families. Dick Whittington spent much of his childhood here. Just to the south, **Cowley** church stands almost against Cowley Manor, now a residential training centre.

Daglingworth: Holy Rood.

The church is in the Duntisbourne valley north-west of Cirencester. Although the interior has been restored, Saxon sculptures remain to show that this is an early church site. These very clear stone carvings are set in the walls and include St Peter and his keys, Christ with hand raised in blessing at the Last Judgement and Christ on the cross with two Roman soldiers holding the spear and pot of vinegar.

Deerhurst: Odda's Chapel. English Heritage.

Deerhurst is beside the Severn downstream from Tewkesbury. It is remarkable for possessing two Saxon churches. Odda's Chapel is just 200 yards (183 metres) south-west of St Mary's Priory. It became incorporated into a Tudor farmhouse known as Abbots Court and was not discovered until 1885. The chancel arch is clearly Saxon, as are the long and short quoins of this rectangular building. It was dated by the inscribed Odda Stone which had been found in a nearby orchard in 1675. This recorded that in 1056 Earl Odda dedicated a royal hall to the Holy Trinity for the good of the soul of his brother Elfric who had died at Deerhurst three years before. Odda was a friend of Edward the Confessor and governed a large area of south-west England.

Deerhurst: St Mary's Priory.
There was a church at Deerhurst in the seventh century or even earlier. It became an important monastery of the lower Severn kingdom of Hwicce and retained its importance at the time when Canute signed a treaty here with Edmund Ironside in 1016. Today, St Mary's Priory is the only surviving Anglo-Saxon monastic church in England. The high external walls have herringbone pattern in the stonework and the long and short quoins of the west tower show that it is mainly Saxon. Inside, the Saxon tub font is said to be the finest in England. High up in the west wall of the nave is a double-headed Saxon window which may contain reused Roman stones.

All Saints church, Down Ampney.

Below this, the middle of three doorways has two fierce animal-headed label stops dating from about AD 804. A famous carving known as the Deerhurst Angel is on a surviving arch of the Saxon apse and is of ninth-century date. The layout of the church was much altered in Saxon times, and again in the fourteenth and fifteenth centuries, when the well carved arches of the nave and clerestory windows were added.

Down Ampney: All Saints.
Situated next to parkland on the south side of the sprawling village, this mainly thirteenth-century church has a solid tower supporting a fourteenth-century spire. The interior was restored by the Victorians but retains its atmosphere. The wooden rood screen, pulpit, reredos and screen to the south transept were designed by Charles Ponting and carved by Harry Hems of Exeter after 1898. In the south transept, two effigies under an arch are of Sir Nicholas de Valers, a crusader, and possibly his wife. There is also a window in remembrance of Arthur Vaughan Williams, who was vicar here when his son Ralph, the famous composer, was born in 1872. The north transept is the Hungerford Chapel, containing a monument of 1637 to Sir John and his son Anthony Hungerford, owners of neighbouring Down Ampney House. A Jacobean screen incorporates fragments of a musicians' gallery from Cirencester Abbey. Against the north exterior of the church, the RAF Garden of Remembrance is in memory of those who served at Down Ampney in 1939-45. Other Ampney churches to the north are worth visiting, such as at **Ampney Crucis.**

Duntisbourne Abbots: St Peter.
This is a Norman church on a Saxon foundation. The low saddleback tower has stone lattice belfry lights added in the thirteenth century. It was much restored by the Victorians, who built an unusual chancel arch supported on double pillars on each side. There is a pleasant sloping churchyard surrounded by cottages.

Duntisbourne Rouse: St Michael.
In this tiny valleyside church in a tranquil setting there is a Saxon doorway and herringbone-patterned walling. Inside, there are thirteenth-century wall paintings with a decorative pattern and misericords believed to have come from Cirencester Abbey. The small saddleback tower was added in 1587.

The Norman chancel arches, Elkstone church.

Elkstone: St John.

An excellent Norman church, its double chancel arches have zigzag decoration, with the outer arches ending in carved beasts' heads. A vaulted chancel lies beyond. The south porch has an arch decorated with zigzags and beaked heads, over a fine tympanum depicting Christ in Majesty. This dates from about 1160. Outside, there are corbel heads along the north and south nave walls. Gargoyles with arms lean out from the corners of the rebuilt tower.

Cat tombstone in the churchyard at Fairford.

English Bicknor: St Mary.

High up above the Wye valley at the north end of the Forest of Dean, this church's Norman origins are indicated by the font and round-columned arcades. There are also some early fourteenth-century stone figures. Grassy paths lead to it through a churchyard of gravestones and table-top tombs. Over the churchyard wall on the south side can be seen the earthworks of a Norman motte and bailey castle.

Fairford: St Mary.

A rich wool and cloth merchant, John Tame, rebuilt this fine church by 1497. Unfinished work was completed by his son, Sir Edmund Tame. The fine central tower has figures carved at the corners, but the church is most noted for its original 28 windows of stained glass, which tell biblical stories all around the church. The great west window shows a spectacular Last Judgement, full of detail. 69 stone corbel angels support the roof timbers of the nave and chancel. The Lady Chapel has the founder's tomb of Purbeck marble beneath a screen separating it from the chancel. On the top are the brasses of John Tame and his wife Alice (died 1500 and 1471). There are wall brasses of Sir Edmund Tame and his two wives. The Lygon tomb here has stone effigies of Katherine and Roger Lygon, dated

1560. The choirstalls have amusing misericords worth examining. Outside the large churchyard has good gravestones, including one opposite the south porch inscribed to Tiddles the church cat, 1963-80.

Gloucester Cathedral: St Peter.

Of great architectural interest, this was a Benedictine abbey church until becoming a cathedral in 1541 after the Dissolution. A monastic house was founded here in AD 681 by Osric, Prince of Mercia, but the present building was begun in 1089. The impressive Norman nave with its great plain round pillars was completed by 1126, and the Early English vaulting above dates from 1242. A large early Norman crypt is below the choir of 1337-60, which has period choirstalls and misericords. The presbytery and transepts were also rebuilt at this time in the Perpendicular style. The great east window of about 1350 is a memorial to local families who fought at the Battle of

The cloisters, Gloucester Cathedral.

Crécy and Siege of Calais in 1346 and 1347, and their heraldic devices can be seen incorporated in the coloured glass. The richly decorated and pinnacled tower was begun in 1450 and is 225 feet (68.6 metres) high. The long and beautifully carved Lady Chapel was added at the close of the fifteenth century and has side chantry chapels with singing galleries. A decorated Norman lead font here came from the ruined Lancaut church beside the Wye.

Monuments in the north ambulatory include the tomb of King Edward II, whose body was carried here by the monks after he was murdered at Berkeley Castle in 1327. The very elaborate tomb and alabaster effigy were ordered by his son, Edward III. Here is also a stone tomb canopy and effigy of Osric, who lies holding a model of the church he founded. This tomb was erected by the last abbot, William Parker, whose own tomb is nearby but does not contain his body. The south ambulatory has a fine wooden effigy of Robert, Duke of Normandy, the eldest son of William the Conqueror. This dates from the mid thirteenth century and lies on a later mortuary chest. Monuments in the nave include a statue of Edward Jenner, the pioneer of the smallpox vaccine, while the prison reformer Sir George Onesiphorus Paul (died 1820) is remembered with a white marble bust on a sarcophagus.

The chapter house retains its original Norman roof and is believed to be the site where William the Conqueror held his Christmas Council in 1085 and ordered the Domesday survey. The Great Cloister is rightly said to be the most beautiful in Britain, with its early carved fan vaulting of 1351-1412. The monks' arched study recesses (carrels) can be seen in the south walk, and their washing place (lavatorium) is perfectly preserved in the north walk. The cloister glass includes some from Prinknash, the country home of the later abbots. The abbey well and drain are in the cloister garth. To the north of the cloister, the arches of the old infirmary stand in the grounds of the King's School. Visitors can also see the treasury and an exhibition depicting the history of the cathedral.

Gloucester: St Mary de Crypt.

The Church is in Southgate Street, where its flat-topped central tower is easily recognised. The original church was built in about 1100, perhaps on Roman foundations, but it was rebuilt in the fifteenth century in the Perpendicular style and restored by the Victorians.

Newland church is the 'cathedral of the forest'.

His conspirator son Francis (1554-84) was executed at Tyburn after being caught aiding the cause of Mary, Queen of Scots. Sir Nicholas (1515-71) was a diplomat who was sent to the Tower for 'encouraging' the marriage of this Mary to the Duke of Norfolk. His daughter Elizabeth married Sir Walter Raleigh.

Newland: All Saints.

The 'cathedral of the forest' is noted for its elaborately pinnacled tower and the tremendous width and space inside. There are some good effigies, such as those of Robert Wakering (died 1237), the original builder of the church, and Jenkin Wyrall (died 1457). Sir John and Lady Joce (died 1344 and 1362) lie on their tomb together. One tomb slab has the brasses of John and Joan Greyndour (died 1443 and 1485), with an additional brass showing a Dean miner carrying his pick and candle. A bowman is crudely inscribed on another slab. The churchyard has several unusual tombs. To the south is a row of almshouses, for eight men and eight women, with a 'habitation adjoining for a lecturer', founded in 1615 by

The tall nave has the original pulpit from which the evangelist George Whitefield first preached on 27th June 1736. This Gloucester man was baptised in the font here, as was Robert Raikes, the founder of the Sunday school movement. The Perpendicular-style chancel is noted for its divided (ogee) arches and wall paintings. The reredos of Venetian mosaic dates from 1889. Brasses in the north transept are of John and Joan Cooke, who founded the Crypt School next door. This was erected in 1539 and later restored in 1880 as a school in memory of Robert Raikes. It is now the church hall. Beside it, Marylane leads to the ruins of Greyfriars church.

Hewelsfield: St Mary Magdalene.

This church on the edge of the Forest of Dean stands within a circular churchyard, which suggests an early date for the site. There are traces of Saxon stonework, but the church is mainly Norman, with a low central tower and an unusual broad west end. Extensive repairs were undertaken in 1971-85. Members of the Throckmorton family are buried here, including Sir John (died 1580), a judge.

Northleach church from the east.

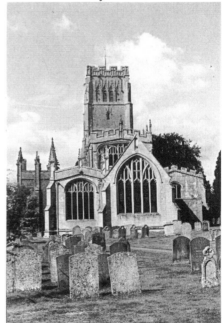

All Saints church, North Cerney.

William Jones of the Worshipful Company of Haberdashers of London. To the west of the church is Newland House.

North Cerney: All Saints.

Norman work here includes the zigzag-decorated south doorway and the base of the saddleback tower, although the church is a Saxon foundation. The nave roof is supported on finely carved corbel heads, and those on the north side are believed to be of Henry VI, William Whitchurch (who rebuilt the church) and the Duke of Buckingham. The Lady Chapel in the south transept has window glass of about 1470 with designs including the sun badge of York. The north transept is a chapel to St Catherine, the patron saint of wool merchants. Fittings include a stone wineglass pulpit of about 1480 and a reading desk dated 1631, while the oak rood loft and the screen into the Lady Chapel were designed by F. C. Eden in the early twentieth century. The Georgian gallery has external stairs. On the outside walls of the Lady Chapel and tower are scratched carvings of a leopard and a manticore (half beast and half human). The church stands across the Churn valley from the attractive North Cerney village.

Northleach: St Peter and St Paul.

This wool church has a tower of about 1350 and a tall nave with clerestory built about a century later. The pinnacled and noble south porch of about 1480 has niches for carvings of saints, the Virgin Mary and Trinity. Grotesques include a cat fiddling to rats. A room over the porch was perhaps for a priest. Inside, the nave's tall concave-sided columns and a great window over the chancel arch are similar to those at Chipping Campden. The delicately carved stone pulpit on a slender stem is of the same period. Much of the church was financed by the woolman John Fortey (died 1458), whose brass shows his feet on a woolpack and sheep. The church is noted for its many other good brasses of local wool merchants of the fifteenth and sixteenth centuries, one of the more elaborate being of Thomas and John Bushe, dated 1525.

Oddington: St Nicholas.

The church at Lower Oddington was restored in 1912, having been disused for sixty years. Its north wall is noted for a large and detailed fourteenth-century Doom or Last Judgement wall painting, executed with great imagination. Across the Evenlode river, the church at **Daylesford** is the resting place of Warren Hastings of Indian fame.

Painswick: St Mary.

The churchyard is famous for its 99 clipped yews and fine table-top tombs which reflect the riches which wool brought to the town's clothiers from the sixteenth century onwards (see chapter 9). A tall spire was added to the

29

Yews and table-top tombs in Painswick churchyard.

church tower in 1632. When struck by lightning in 1883, the top 40 feet (12 metres) fell through the nave roof and damaged several tombs. Inside the church, the north aisle of 1377-99 is of special interest. Of the corbel heads supporting the roof timbers, the two nearest St Peter's Chapel are Richard II and his queen, Anne of Bohemia. The chapel contains a Purbeck-marble tomb used three times, first for Viscount Lisle in 1356, then for Sir William Kingston in 1540 and lastly for Dr John Seaman in 1621. The figures of Seaman and his wife kneel towards three books supporting a column. The tomb was moved here from the chancel in 1743. At the west end of the aisle hangs a model of Sir Francis Drake's ship *Bonaventure*, which fought the Spanish Armada.

Prinknash Abbey

The world-famous abbey at Prinknash, pronounced 'Prinage', was completed in 1972 to a modern design and clad in Guiting stone from the Cotswolds. At present, its eight bells are held outside in a temporary structure. Guided tours of the monastery can be arranged, although most visitors come to see the pottery and bird park (chapter 8). The 300 acre

(121 ha) Prinknash Park is in a splendid setting on the Cotswold edge and contains St Peter's Grange, now a retreat and conference centre but open to the public over two fortnights each year. It was a manor house with a chapel, rebuilt from a hunting lodge by William Parker, the last Benedictine abbot of Gloucester. After the Dissolution it was the residence of various families, including the Bridgemans, who were here in 1643 when Prince Rupert made it his headquarters during the siege of Gloucester. Finally, in 1888 the property was bought by Thomas Dyer Edwarde. When he became a Catholic in 1924, he invited the Benedictines of Caldey Island to re-establish a monastery at Prinknash Park. Four years later, the manor house became their abbey. The new abbey was begun in 1939 but the work was not finished for another 33 years.

Quenington: St Swithin.

The church is famous for its two richly carved Norman doorways. The tympanum over the north doorway shows the Harrowing of Hell, while there is a ram's head carved above the arch. The south doorway has the Coronation of the Virgin, with the four evangelists represented by an angel, eagle, lion and bull. The otherwise plain church has a bell turret in place of a tower. It is in the south-east corner of the village near the gatehouse of Quenington Court, an establishment of the Knights Hospitallers.

Rendcomb: St Peter.

This late fifteenth-century wool church was financed by Sir Edmund Tame, who completed his father's work at Fairford church. It has a very fine Norman font with carvings of eleven apostles and a blank left for Judas. Of the Norman church, there are three columns revealed in the north wall of the nave. There is a restored sixteenth-century screen. The church is close to Rendcomb College, an Italianate-style boys' public school, designed in the 1860s by Philip Hardwick.

Sapperton: St Kenelm.

This interesting cruciform church was rebuilt by the Atkyns family in the early eighteenth century. The south transept has a very elaborate canopied tomb of Sir Robert Atkyns, the county historian, who died of dysentery at his Westminster house in 1711, and his wife, Louise, who died five years later. In the north transept, the kneeling figures of Sir Henry Poole (died 1616) and his wife Anne are surrounded by their children in another splendid monument. Woodwork in the church came from the Atkynses' manor house, such as the Jacobean caryatids which stand at the door of each of the box-pews, and the small gallery over the south porch. Ernest Gimson and the Barnsley brothers, who had their craft workshops at Daneway House, are buried in the sloping churchyard.

Selsley: All Saints.

The church dates from the 1860s, when it was designed by the architect G. F. Bodley and financed by Sir Samuel Marling. Its tall saddleback tower can be seen on the edge of Selsley Common high above Marling's Ebley Mill (see chapter 7) in the Stroud valley. It is famous for the stained glass windows, which were among the earliest commissions for William Morris and Company, their designers including William Morris, Dante Gabriel Rossetti, Ford Madox Brown and Sir Edward Burne-Jones.

Southrop: St Peter.

This small church tucked away in a pretty stone village has no tower. The north and south walls of the nave have a very clear herringbone pattern of late Saxon type. There is a Norman north doorway and low chancel arch. The font is comparable with Rendcomb's, and its detailed carvings include five Virtues trampling on five Vices. John Keble was curate here in 1823-5.

Tetbury: St Mary.

This large church was built by Francis Hiorn in 1781 and was one of the earliest Gothic Revival churches. Of its medieval predecessor, only the tower and spire were retained until they were rebuilt in 1891. The spire is 186 feet (57 metres) high and makes a landmark for the town from afar. The church is tall, with large windows and very slender wooden columns which support the plaster ceiling. Even more unusual are the narrow ambulatories down the sides of the building, with doors to give access to the box-pews.

The modern Prinknash Abbey, completed in 1972.

Tewkesbury Abbey: St Mary.

There were monks at Tewkesbury by AD 715, but the present abbey church was founded by Robert Fitzhamon in about 1087 and completed in 1121. The Benedictine abbey was dissolved in 1539 and the church was bought by the people of Tewkesbury to become one of the largest parish churches in Britain. The nave and transepts are Norman, as is the 132 foot (40 metre) central tower, visible from miles away. The west front has a recessed Norman arch, the largest of its type in Britain. The window is later, of 1686. Inside, plain round Norman pillars support the fourteenth-century vaulting of the nave. The choir windows have stained glass dating from 1330-40. The abbey is second only to Westminster Abbey in the number of medieval monuments, notably the very fine chantries around the ambulatory. The Founder's Chantry was built by Abbot Parker in about 1397 over the tomb of Robert Fitzhamon, who died in 1107. The Despenser Tomb was built in 1349 for Hugh, Baron Despenser, and his wife, who financed the chapels around the choir and the vaulting of the whole church. Their alabaster effigies lie beneath a canopy which is said to be the finest in existence, although its 26 statues were destroyed during the Commonwealth period. The tomb of Hugh le Despenser had 41 statues. He was hung, drawn and quartered at Hereford in 1326, and his remains were buried here. A large Purbeck-marble tomb of Abbot John Cotes (died 1347) was incorporated in the tomb in the seventeenth century. The Chapel of the Holy Trinity is the chantry tomb of Sir Edward Despenser (died 1375), who was standard-bearer to the Black Prince. His effigy kneels on top, facing the high altar. There are tombs of abbots, the most interesting being the Wakeman Cenotaph with an elaborate canopy. It shows a decaying corpse with a mouse, snake, worm and frog in attendance. This was intended for John Wakeman, the last abbot, who became the first Bishop of Gloucester in September 1541. A small wall monument by the south transept is to Dinah Maria Mulock (1826-87), the Mrs Craik who wrote *John Halifax, Gentleman*, a book which features Tewkesbury and other places in the county. Beyond the west end of the church can be seen the Abbey Gateway, while the Abbey Mill (chapter 7) is on the site of the monastic mill.

Tewkesbury Abbey from the south-west.

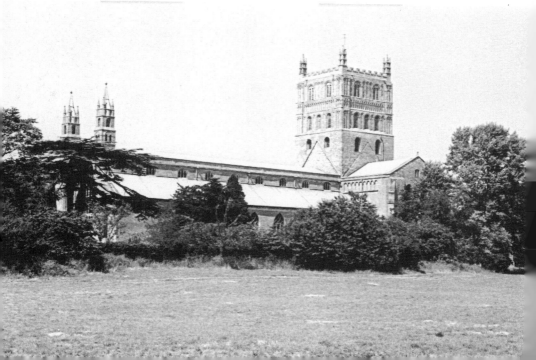

Ashleworth Tithe Barn and church.

5
Historic buildings and gardens

Some houses and gardens are open only at limited times, so it is always worth checking before planning a visit. Other gems, not listed here, are open even less frequently. Gloucestershire has surprisingly few castles but it is often possible to see sites on private property from nearby. Such is the substantial ruin of **Beverston Castle** near Tetbury, part incorporated in a house but prominent beside the village church. Motte and bailey earthworks can be seen from churches or their approaches, as at **Brimpsfield** and **English Bicknor** (chapter 4).

Ashleworth Tithe Barn, Ashleworth. National Trust.

This fifteenth-century tithe barn stands near Ashleworth church on the west bank of the Severn. It is 120 feet (36.6 metres) long and has two projecting porch bays and a stone-tiled roof. There are impressive roof timbers within.

Barnsley House Garden, Barnsley, near Cirencester. Telephone: 028574 281.

The garden, redesigned by Rosemary Verey and her late husband, David, since 1960, includes a variety of features such as the laburnum walk, the rock-rose walk, a knot garden and a formally designed kitchen garden. In the main garden are an original Gothick summerhouse and a classical temple, both of the eighteenth century. Barnsley House (1697) is not open.

Batsford Arboretum, near Moreton-in-Marsh. Telephone: 0386 700409.

The arboretum was laid out at Batsford Park in the 1880s by Lord Redesdale. Having returned from a posting in Tokyo, he brought a Japanese flavour to his work such as a bronze Buddha and deer, and a rest house which was built to a Japanese design. The spring and autumn colours are especially beautiful, although there is much to see in the summer including vistas from the upper garden over the Evenlode valley. There is also a garden centre (open all year) and the Cotswold Falconry, Eagle and Hawk Park (telephone: 0386 701043), which has daily flying displays.

Berkeley Castle, Berkeley GL13 9BQ. Telephone: 0453 810332.

The Berkeley family has lived here since 1153, when their ancestor Robert FitzHarding built a Norman shell-keep around an earlier mound. Massive buttresses support the keep and surrounding curtain wall, within which were added buildings in the fourteenth century. The castle was made notorious by the imprisonment and treacherous murder of Edward II here in 1327. Thomas, Lord Berkeley, was host at the time, although he may have played no part in the deed, which took place in the room known as the King's Gallery. The 62 foot (19 metre) long Great Hall was built in about 1340. It was repaired in 1497 but the original roof timbers remain. A sixteenth-century painted screen is at one end, while tapestries depicting the history of Queen Esther hang on the walls. Other, Brussels tapestries hang in the Morning Room, which was once a chapel of St Mary. Drake's Room is so called because it was often used by Sir Francis Drake on his journeys to and from the Forest of Dean (of which he was Warden). His ebony furniture from the Portuguese East Indies can be seen in the Tower Room. Portraits in the dining room include those of Sir William Berkeley, who became Governor of Virginia in 1641, and George Berkeley, Bishop of Cloyne, the benefactor of Berkeley University, California. Other rooms on view include the long and small drawing rooms and the beer cellar, where beer was brewed and stored in the nineteenth and early twentieth centuries. The castle suffered no great damage when it was captured by the Parliamentarians after a three-day siege in the Civil War. The exterior can be viewed from the garden which features terraces and grass walks.

Blackfriars Priory, off Ladybellegate Street, Gloucester. Telephone: 0452 27688. English Heritage.

This is said to be the best preserved medi-eval Dominican friary in Britain. After the Dissolution, the thirteenth-century church was converted to a private mansion by Alderman Thomas Bell. Much of the original timber roof survives in the hall. Almost opposite, across Southgate Street, can be seen the arcade of the ruined nave and north aisle of the early sixteenth-century **Greyfriars church**. It stands behind Greyfriars House, built in about 1800 and now a library. Another ruin is the Augustinian **St Oswald's Priory**, where there is a standing wall with arches and a plan of other walls laid out in a park off Archdeacon Street.

Chavenage, near Tetbury. Telephone: 0666 502329.

This Elizabethan house stands on the site of a much earlier manor which was owned by Augustinian monks until the Dissolution. Edward Stephens reconstructed and enlarged the house in 1576, and his initials and date can be seen over the porch. The main hall has notable tall windows and a screen forming a minstrels' gallery. Several rooms contain tapestries, furniture and relics of the Cromwellian period. Colonel Nathaniel Stephens, who was related to Oliver Cromwell by marriage, was a moderate Member of Parliament for Gloucestershire in the Civil War. It took two attempts by Cromwell and Henry Ireton to persuade him to vote for the impeachment of the captured King Charles I. When he agreed after much argument, his daughter

Berkeley Castle.

Frocester Tithe Barn.

Abigail swore he would suffer an awful penance and he died within a few months after a long illness. Cromwell's and Ireton's Rooms are believed to be where these men lodged, and Queen Anne's Room recalls another visitor. Other rooms include the library, billiards room and dining room. The ballroom was added in 1904, with a sprung dance floor of Canadian maple. The chapel is very close to the house and contains a Saxon font found in the structure of a barn on the estate.

Cirencester Park, Cecily Hill, Cirencester.
This large park of 3000 acres (1200 ha) begins close to the town centre of Cirencester,

and the public has access to long woodland drives and walks. Polo is played here every Sunday during the summer.

Frocester Tithe Barn, Frocester Court, near Stonehouse, Stroud. Telephone: 045382 3250.
This large tithe barn stands in a small farming hamlet lying below the Coaley Peak Picnic Site and viewpoint (chapter 2). The nearby Tudor gatehouse and courthouse complete the scene.

Hailes Abbey ruins, Stanway, near Winchcombe, Cheltenham GL54 5PB. Telephone: 0242 602398. National Trust and

Hailes Abbey.

CHAPTER 5

English Heritage.

This was among the last Cistercian abbeys, founded in 1246 by Richard, Earl of Cornwall, who had pledged to do so if he survived danger at sea. The land at the foot of the Cotswolds was given by his brother Henry III, who attended the dedication in 1251 with his queen Eleanor, Richard and thirteen bishops. Much of the abbey's wealth was derived from wool and the pilgrims who came to see a phial containing the blood of Christ (later proved a fake), presented by Richard's son Edmund in 1270. Chaucer referred to the phial in the *Pardoner's Tale*. The abbey was the twelfth richest Cistercian house in England when it was dissolved on Christmas Eve 1539. The abbey church was demolished, but the abbot's lodging and west range became a house before they were also demolished in the early eighteenth century. Some stone found its way to Stanway church, where it is now set in the north churchyard wall.

Of the ruins today, the cloister is the best preserved, with several arches still standing. In the outline of the abbey church it can be seen where the east end was extended beyond the altar to house the shrine of the holy blood, with an apse from which radiated five chapels, a feature known as a chevet. South of the cloister, other foundations include the monks' frater and undercroft. The reredorter or latrine

was flushed by the main drain, which can be seen still flowing with water. There is a good museum here containing examples of carved stones and other relics (see chapter 6). Across the road, the small twelfth-century **Hailes church** has medieval wall paintings, notably a large figure of St Christopher and a hunting scene with a hunter and three hounds cornering a hare or rabbit.

Hidcote Manor Garden, Hidcote Bartrim, Mickleton, near Chipping Campden GL55 6LR. Telephone: 0386 438333. National Trust.

This wonderful garden was the creation of the horticulturalist Major Lawrence Johnston over a period of forty years from 1907. Walls and hedges separate a series of small formal and informal gardens, famous for rare shrubs, trees, herbaceous borders and old roses. Gazebos, pools and distant views complete the scene. Open-air plays are performed on the Theatre Lawn in July.

Kiftsgate Court Gardens, Mickleton, near Chipping Campden GL55 6LW. Telephone: 0386 438777.

Kiftsgate is on a wooded slope with fine views opposite Hidcote Manor Garden. The gardens are sheltered by hedges and have many unusual plants and shrubs. They are

Hidcote Manor Garden.

Kingswood Abbey Gatehouse.

famous for old-fashioned rose bushes includ-ing the 'Rose Filipes Kiftsgate', claimed to be the largest rose in England.

Kingswood Abbey Gatehouse, Abbey Street, Kingswood, near Wotton-under-Edge. Eng-lish Heritage.

The fifteenth-century gatehouse is all that survives of the Cistercian abbey, with wings on either side, one a ruin and the other a house. The room above the arch possesses a window with interesting stonework.

Littledean Hall, Littledean, near Cinderford GL14 3NR. Telephone: 0594 824213.

This was originally the medieval manor of Dene. It is said to be the oldest inhabited house in England, for part of the cellar contains the remains of a Saxon-type hall which used Ro-man material from a site nearby. This became the undercroft of a Norman hall, which in turn was added to in later centuries. Much of the house was rebuilt when Charles Bridgeman bought it in 1612, so that earlier work is heavily disguised. It was altered again several times until 1852, when the present 'Jacobean' front was added. The house is under restora-tion and the tour concentrates on ghosts, for several parts are reputed to be haunted. One place is the dining room, where three separate tragedies took place concerning a black serv-ant, two brothers who killed each other, and killings in the Civil War. The library, with an elaborately carved overmantel, is where Prince Maurice planned his campaigns in April 1643. The Blue Bedroom is believed to be where he slept.

Near the house is the site of a recently discovered Roman temple complex, possibly the largest in rural Britain and excavated since 1985. The grounds consist of parkland with ancient chestnuts, and the Panorama Walk passes the Norman earthwork known as the Old Castle of Dene and a superb viewpoint across the great horseshoe bend of the Severn at Newnham.

Llanthony Priory, Llanthony Road, Gloucester. Gloucester City Museums. Tele-phone: 0452 24131.

Fugitive monks founded a priory here in 1136 after Welsh rebels took their priory of the same name in the Black Mountains. The church was rebuilt in the thirteenth century and in 1493-1513, this last time by prior Henry Dene, a member of Henry VII's Council who became Archbishop of Canterbury in 1501. The priory was the seventh richest Augustin-ian house in England when it was dissolved in 1538. The property became a family estate, and the church and cloister were destroyed during the Civil War period. The remaining 5 acre (2 ha) site of the outer and inner courts is a welcome contrast to the industrial ware-houses which surround it. The surviving structures include part of the outer gatehouse (1494-1500), the precinct wall, two ruined ranges of the outer court and a buttressed barn of the fifteenth century. At present under restoration is a half-timbered range with a roof which is attached to a brick-built farmhouse of 1880. A cattle pond of 1860 is now a nature reserve.

Lydney Park Gardens, Lydney GL15 6BU. Telephone: 0594 842844.

Lydney Park belonged to the Royalist Wintour family but has been owned by the Bathursts and their descendants since 1723. The late Victorian house (not open) is now the home of Lord Bledisloe, whose father created magnificent gardens with magnolias, rhodo-dendrons, azaleas and other flowering shrubs. These are in a sheltered valley behind the house, landscaped with lakes and a stream. Visitors may also picnic in the deer park,

St Briavels Castle.

Sezincote.

which has a herd of fallow deer. Of additional interest are the Roman temple, iron age hillfort and Roman and New Zealand Museums in the house (chapters 3 and 6). The gardens are open for a limited season only.

Misarden Park Gardens, Miserden, Stroud GL6 7JA. Telephone: 028582 303.

Misarden Park is at Miserden, 3 miles (5 km) north-east of Bisley. The house (not open) dates from 1620, with nineteenth-century additions and a wing of the 1920s by Sir Edwin Lutyens. Around it are the gardens, remodelled in the 1930s and after to include a rose garden, with recent introductions, herbaceous borders, shrubbery, arboretum and lawns. The yew hedges of the Yew Walk and Butler's Walk are notable features. Plants are for sale at the garden nurseries. The gardens have limited opening, but the Woodland Trail in the Frome valley is open daily. This takes in a variety of tree species, a lake and river and passes the earthworks of a Norman motte and bailey castle (no access).

Newark Park, Ozleworth, Wotton-under-Edge GL12 7PZ. Telephone: 0453 842644.

National Trust.

The house stands on the edge of a cliff and was built by the Poyntz family as an Elizabethan hunting lodge. It was later converted to a castellated country house by James Wyatt in 1790. The house and grounds have been rehabilitated by the tenant, Mr R. L. Parsons, and lie 1 1/2 miles (2 km) east of Wotton-under-Edge.

Painswick Rococo Garden, The Stables, Painswick House, Painswick GL6 6TH. Telephone: 0452 813204.

This 6 acre (2.4 ha) valley garden is a very rare complete example of the rococo style of garden design dating from the mid eighteenth century. It combines the formal features seen in earlier gardens with the more natural elements which became popular in the eighteenth century. Included in the general asymmetrical pattern is a variety of garden buildings. The garden is being restored to its layout as illustrated in a painting of 1748 by Thomas Robins.

St Briavels Castle, St Briavels.

The castle and attractive stone village stand high up with glimpses of the wooded Wye

Painswick Rococo Garden.

valley. The constable of the castle was Warden of the Forest of Dean and Norman kings stayed here when hunting. The original castle was built in 1131 by Milo Fitz Walter, Earl of Hereford, but the remains today date from the mid thirteenth century. Most of the curtain wall stands and a garden has been made in the dry moat. The two robust round towers of the gatehouse became a debtors' prison in 1670-1720 but are now part of a youth hostel. Opposite, St Mary's church has Norman and Early English work but was much restored in 1861. The villagers' rights to the woodlands are affirmed in an ancient bread and cheese ceremony held in May.

Sezincote, near Moreton-in-Marsh GL56 9AW.

The water garden is overlooked by an Indian temple and contains trees of unusual size and diversity. It was laid out around 1805 using some of Humphry Repton's ideas but the Indian Garden south of the house was created in 1968. The house was built for Sir Charles Cockerell, by his brother and Thomas Daniell. It features oriental arches and onion domes, with a pinnacled north wing and orangery, and was the inspiration for the Brighton Pavilion. The gardens are open more frequently than the house.

Snowshill Manor, Snowshill, near Broadway, Worcestershire WR12 7JU. Telephone: 0386 852410. National Trust.

A Tudor manor house of about 1500, with a façade added two hundred years later, all in local stone, Snowshill was originally owned by Winchcombe Abbey. Its dark interior is filled with the late Charles Wade's large collection of craftsmanship, including musical instruments, toys, dolls, bicycles, clocks, weavers' and spinners' tools and Japanese

Snowshill Manor from the garden.

39

samurai armour. Outside, there is a small terraced cottage garden, with a dovecote and the Priest's House where Charles Wade lived. The small village of Snowshill sits high above a coomb, with a village green and a restored church.

Stanway House, Stanway, Cheltenham GL54 5PQ. Telephone: 038673 469.

This fine Jacobean manor house of mellowed golden stone was built in 1580-1630, with later alterations. The Great Hall dates from around 1600 and has a screens passage and minstrels' gallery. Unusual furniture includes a pair of Chippendale day beds of about 1760 in the drawing room. Many family portraits adorn this and other rooms, such as the Old Library and Elcho Sitting Room. The Audit Room is of interest, as rents are still received here from estate tenants in the traditional manner. The Pyramid was erected on a hill behind the house in 1750 in memory of John Tracy. The landscaped grounds contain an ice house and a dog cemetery. A fourteenth-century tithe barn here was built for Tewkesbury Abbey, which had owned the manor since the early eighth century. The Tracy family acquired the manor from the abbey in 1533, and it came by marriage in 1817 to the Earls of Wemyss. The magnificent three-storeyed gatehouse is decorated with scallop shells, the insignia of the Tracys, and is believed to have been designed by Timothy Strong of Barrington in about 1630. It stands next to the church (St Peter), much restored in the 1890s, but with some Norman work and fragments of carved stone from Hailes Abbey built into the churchyard wall.

Sudeley Castle and Gardens, Winchcombe, Cheltenham GL54 5JD. Telephone: 0242 604357 or 602308.

Little remains of the original castle built during the civil war between Stephen and Matilda, for it was rebuilt in the fifteenth century by Ralph Botelar, Baron of Sudeley and Lord Chamberlain. Of his work there survive outer and inner courts on the north and south ranges and a great barn. Sudeley became a royal castle when it was confiscated by Edward IV, for Botelar supported the Lancastrians. Later, Richard III used the castle and his ruined apartments can still be seen. Henry VIII stayed here with Katherine of Aragon and Anne Boleyn, but it is mostly celebrated as the home of his widow, Katherine Parr, who mar-

ried Lord Seymour in 1547, a year before she died. The adjoining chapel (St Mary) contains her tomb. When Seymour died, the castle was held for the king by Lord Chandos. The castle was slighted during the Civil War, when the royalist Chandos went over to the Parliamentarians. It was uninhabited until the Dent-Brocklehurst family employed Sir Gilbert Scott to restore Sudeley as a family home in the 1850s. It was Scott who designed the ornate tomb for Katherine Parr now seen in the chapel. The castle contains old masters such as Rubens and Van Dyck, tapestries and many Civil War artefacts. Set in parkland, there are fine formal gardens with clipped yews near the house. The castle and grounds are open to the public. There are also craft workshops, exhibitions and an adventure playground for children.

Westbury Court Garden, Westbury-on-Severn GL14 1PD. Telephone: 045276 461. National Trust.

This formal water garden with canals and yew hedges is the earliest of its kind in England. It was laid out in 1696-1705, when Maynard Colchester completed the 450 foot (137 metre) Long Canal and the Tall Pavilion, a summerhouse. The T Canal, which features a statue of Neptune, was probably completed by Colchester's nephew in about 1715. He also erected a square gazebo and made the adjacent walled garden. The striking Tall Pavilion was incorporated in a house which stood here from 1895 until 1960. Having fallen into decay, the garden was restored in 1971, with the planting of apple, pear and plum trees of varieties pre-dating 1700. The nearby church has a separate broad tower with a massive shingled spire which makes Westbury easy to find from afar.

Westonbirt Arboretum, Westonbirt, near Tetbury GL8 8QS. Telephone: 066688 220. Forestry Commission.

The Forestry Commission maintains this world-famous arboretum, 3 miles (5 km) southwest of Tetbury and right on the Gloucestershire border. It was begun in 1829 by Robert Holford of Westonbirt House, and his son, Sir George Holford, continued the work so that the arboretum matured in the intervening years to become one of the finest in the world. Some of the tree specimens are the largest in Britain. The most popular times to visit are in May and October, when the colours are at their finest. There are good walks through the Silkwood

Stanway gatehouse and church.

part of the property. A visitor centre at the entrance explains the arboretum and the management of woodlands. The whole site covers 600 acres (240 ha).

Whittington Court, Whittington, near Cheltenham GL54 4HF. Telephone: 0242 820218. Limited opening.

This many-gabled Cotswold-stone manor house is said to have been built by Richard Cotton soon after his family purchased the site in 1545. It was probably his son John who entertained Elizabeth I during her progress through Gloucestershire in September 1592. The present hallway is the original east end of the main hall. Oak wall panelling here and in the dining hall was brought from Sevenhampton Manor in the nineteenth century, when the house was owned by the Lawrence family. There are many stone fireplaces, such as a Tudor fireplace in the dining hall, or a notable Renaissance example in the library. This room also has furniture brought from neighbouring Sandywell Park. The great staircase has a seventeenth-century dog gate on the first half-landing, to prevent dogs going upstairs. Outside are a moat and a good farm range with a barn. The church (St Bartholomew) stands right up against the house and contains the effigies of two knights and a lady

of the de Crupes family, who held the manor in the middle ages. Just north is the estate village of mellow-coloured stone cottages.

Woodchester Park Mansion, Nympsfield, near Stroud. Telephone: 0453 860531.

The wealthy Catholic convert William Leigh employed Benjamin Bucknall to design a Gothic-revival monastic house with a chapel and central courtyard. This fantastic Victorian house was begun in 1854 but abandoned in about 1868 and left three-quarters finished with the original scaffolding still in place. Local limestone was used for all the high-quality stonework including the vaulted ceilings, which were completed only in the drawing room and chapel. There are gargoyles, and stone owls supporting the gutters of the servants' range. Of interest is a solid stone bath with stone gargoyles to supply hot and cold water. The Woodchester Mansion Trust has been formed to preserve the south range in its unfinished state as a museum of Victorian quality building techniques. The chapel and other accommodation will be restored and the house will be used for courses on architecture and the training of stonemasons. There are guided tours on open days, when there is access from near the Coaley Peak picnic site (see chapter 2).

Cheltenham: the Pittville Pump Room Museum.

6
Museums and art galleries

There are museums at other sites, such as Chedworth Roman Villa and Clearwell Caves (chapters 3 and 7).

BERKELEY
The Jenner Museum, Church Lane, Berkeley GL13 9BH. Telephone: 0453 810631.

Dr Edward Jenner (1749-1823), the 'Father of Immunology', was born in Berkeley, where his father was vicar, and returned to live and practise as a doctor in this beautiful Georgian house near the castle (see chapter 5) and church. It contains a collection relating to his work on smallpox vaccination, which he pioneered. As well as his medical work he helped launch a hydrogen balloon and studied hedgehogs and cuckoos. He died here and is buried in the church. In the attractive garden is a rustic thatched hut, which he called the Temple of Vaccinia, where he vaccinated local people and the poor free of charge.

BOURTON-ON-THE-WATER
Cotswolds Motor Museum, The Old Mill, Bourton-on-the-Water GL54 2BY. Telephone: 0451 21255.

Here is a fantastic collection in the former corn mill on the river Windrush in the heart of Bourton-on-the-Water. Motor cars and motorcycles, including sporting and touring machines and a 1935 London taxi, are all housed amid one of the largest collections of motoring memorabilia in Britain. This includes Britain's largest display of enamel advertising signs, petrol pumps and signs, a repair shop and even caravans of the 1920s. Children's pedal cars, motorcycles and aeroplanes are also of interest. The **Village Life Exhibition** is in another part of the mill and contains various items, such as a reconstructed blacksmith's forge and village shop. A scale model shows the corn mill when it was working in the 1930s.

CHELTENHAM
Cheltenham Art Gallery and Museum, Clarence Street, Cheltenham GL50 3JT. Telephone: 0242 237431.

A section of the museum covers the social history and development of Cheltenham as a spa town. One room displays personal effects, photographs and watercolours of Dr Edward Wilson, a Cheltenham man, who perished with Scott on the British Antarctic Expedition in 1912. The archaeological collection contains prehistoric and Roman artefacts, including an important hoard of late bronze age metalwork from Nottingham Hill (chapter 3) and two lead cisterns from a Roman site at Bourton-on-the-Water. The art collection contains notable English, Dutch and Flemish paintings from the seventeenth century onwards, and there is a large collection of English and oriental pottery and porcelain. Pride of place is given to a gallery displaying furniture and metalwork of the Arts and Crafts Movement, which thrived in the Cotswolds in the late nineteenth and early twentieth centuries. These include pieces by C. R. Ashbee, C. F. A. Voisey, W. R. Lethaby, Ernest Gimson, the brothers Ernest and Sidney Barnsley, and Peter Waals. There are also regular temporary exhibitions in the Art Gallery and Museum.

Gustav Holst Birthplace Museum, 4 Clarence Road, Pittville, Cheltenham GL52 2AY. Telephone: 0242 524846.

This is a Regency house with rooms furnished variously in Regency, Victorian and Edwardian styles, including a working kitchen and scullery. The composer Gustav Holst was born here in 1874 and displays on his life and music include his piano. Other family items are also exhibited.

Pittville Pump Room Museum, Pittville Park, Cheltenham. Telephone: 0242 512740.

The museum is also known as the Gallery of Fashion, as there are displays of original fashions. Costumed figures are posed in front of painted views depicting the development of Cheltenham from the 1780s to the present day. Photographic panels also tell the history of Cheltenham, Britain's most complete Regency town. Changing jewellery fashions from Regency to Art Nouveau are shown in a room which houses temporary exhibitions of textiles, embroidery and costume. The museum is housed on the upper floors of the Grade I listed Pittville Pump Room, which is magnificently situated overlooking Pittville Park and Lake.

CHIPPING CAMPDEN
Woolstaplers' Hall Museum, High Street, Chipping Campden GL55 6HB. Telephone: 0386 840289.

There is much to see in this museum in a fourteenth-century wool hall. There are displays of items relating to the wool trade, a cobbler's shop, an Edwardian photographic studio, photographic and cinematographic collections and period costumes. The Woolstaplers' Hall itself contains a Victorian balloon and parachute and a large collection of iron and steel mantraps.

CIRENCESTER
Cirencester Lock-up, Trinity Road, Cirencester GL7 1BR. Telephone: 0285 655611.

This is one of the few preserved lock-ups in England open to the public, restored in 1982. There are two cells beneath a curious domed roof, each containing displays on lock-ups and the conservation of historic buildings in the Cotswolds. The lock-up stood in Gloucester Street before it was brought here in 1837 when the Cirencester Union Workhouse was completed. This pleasing two-storey complex in local stone now houses the Cotswold District Council offices. The lock-up key is available from here or the Corinium Museum. Other lock-ups can be seen at Bibury and Bisley.

Corinium Museum, Park Street, Cirencester GL7 2BX. Telephone: 0285 655611.

The museum contains a large collection of Roman artefacts, many from Cirencester itself. These include sculpted tombstones and parts of columns such as a fine capital from a column dedicated to Jupiter. There are many mosaic pavements with themes depicting a hare, hunting dogs, sea gods, dolphins, Venus and Orpheus. There are also reconstructions of a Roman dining room, kitchen and garden. A mosaic maker's shop is of interest, for

The Temple of Vaccinia at the Jenner Museum.

Cirencester: the Roman garden in the Corinium Museum.

Cirencester was the home of the so-called *Corinium* school. Other archaeological material includes a reconstructed neolithic chambered tomb from Hazleton, finds from Saxon warrior graves and fragments from Cirencester Abbey. The museum has changing exhibitions throughout the year.

COLEFORD
Great Western Railway Museum, Railway Drive, Coleford. Telephone: 0594 33569 or 32032.

The museum is housed in the goods station of 1883, on the site of the Coleford railway yard and accessible from the town's main car park. It is one of the few remaining railway buildings in the Forest of Dean. Exhibits include a signal box, scale-model steam locomotives, photographs of the railways of Coleford and the Forest of Dean, and other railway memorabilia.

GLOUCESTER
Beatrix Potter Shop and Museum, The House of the Tailor of Gloucester, 9 College Court, Gloucester GL1 2NJ. Telephone: 0452 422856.

This tiny shop next to St Michael's Gate into the cathedral close was chosen by Beatrix Potter as the tailor's home in her famous book *The Tailor of Gloucester*. There are many exhibits relating to the life and work of Beatrix Potter and the shop sells gifts based on her favourite characters.

City East Gate, Eastgate Street, Gloucester.

An exhibition chamber beneath Boots the Chemist preserves part of the foundations of Gloucester's East Gate and the adjoining city wall and ditch. Both Roman and medieval stonework can be seen here.

Gloucester City Museum and Art Gallery, Brunswick Road, Gloucester GL1 1HP. Telephone: 0452 24131.

The ground floor of this late Victorian building contains displays on natural history and archaeology. Of special note is a decorated bronze mirror which was found with other grave goods in an iron age burial at Birdlip. There are many Roman stone carvings and sculptures from the city and elsewhere in Gloucestershire. A section of the Roman city wall is exposed beneath the floor. Good examples of Anglo-Saxon sculptures include two elaborately carved cross sections from St Oswald's Priory. The Gloucester Tables Set of bone and antler is the oldest known backgammon set and was found in

1971 on the site of William I's Gloucester Castle. Upstairs, there are displays of fine furniture, pottery, glass and silver. Among the coins on show is the Painswick Hoard of 34 gold and eight silver coins, apparently hidden for safety in about 1644. There are paintings by Turner and Gainsborough, and a view of Gloucester by Johannes Vorsterman must show the appearance of the city shortly after the great Civil War siege.

Gloucester Folk Museum, 99-103 Westgate Street, Gloucester GL1 2PG. Telephone: 0452 26467.

This excellent museum is housed in three timber-framed houses of the late fifteenth and early seventeenth centuries, traditionally known as Bishop Hooper's Lodging, and new extensions. Displays are as diverse as a nineteenth-century wheelwright's shop, a shoemaker's workshop, a late Victorian schoolroom, agricultural implements, dairying equipment (including large presses for cheesemaking), Severn estuary eel and salmon fishing equipment, old toys and games, the remains of the city's South Gate and the supposed base of the stake at which Bishop John Hooper was burnt in 1555. There is also a programme of special exhibitions. The floors of the old buildings are remarkable for their unevenness. The upper floor was once a pin factory and equipment is on display as well as the original forge.

Gloucester Transport Museum, Bearland, Gloucester. Telephone: 0452 26467.

This small museum is in a former fire station and the collection can be viewed through the glass doors. It includes a horse-drawn fire engine of about 1895 and a tram of about 1880, a Gloucestershire wagon, Dursley Pedersen cycles and a Morris one-ton commercial vehicle of 1926.

Museum of Advertising and Packaging, Albert Warehouse, Gloucester Docks, Gloucester GL1 2EH. Telephone: 0452 302309.

This interesting museum houses the Robert Opie Collection of Advertising and Packaging, the largest of its type in the world. Memories are easily aroused by the sight of all those once so familiar tins, packets and bottles which were usually thrown away. The development of packaging and labelling is clearly demonstrated in the displays. A more modern aspect of advertising is the screening of early television commercials. The Albert Warehouse was built in 1851 and is just one part of the revitalised Gloucester Docks complex.

National Waterways Museum, Llanthony Warehouse, Gloucester Docks, Gloucester GL1 2EH. Telephone: 0452 307009 or 25524.

The great seven-storey Llanthony Warehouse contains imaginative displays which tell the story of Britain's waterways. There are

The National Waterways Museum is housed in a fine warehouse in Gloucester Docks.

Newent: the Shambles Museum.

working models, exhibits, archive films, sound recordings and craft demonstrations. Llanthony Yard is recreated in the form of a canal maintenance yard with workshops where craftsmen such as blacksmiths demonstrate their work. The collection of historic boats moored in the dock alongside includes narrow boats and the working Number 4 steam dredger of 1927. Various events and exhibitions are held throughout the year.

Regiments of Gloucestershire Museum, Custom House, Commercial Road, Gloucester GL1 2HE. Telephone: 0452 22682.

The museum is in the nineteenth-century Custom House between Gloucester Docks and Commercial Road. It tells the history of the Gloucestershire Regiment and the Royal Gloucestershire Hussars in times of war and peace since 1694, including their campaigns in the Peninsular War, the North African desert, France and Korea. There are reconstructed scenes, uniform displays, photographs of living conditions of soldiers and their families, archive film and sound effects.

HAILES
Hailes Abbey Museum, near Winchcombe, Cheltenham GL54 5PB. Telephone: 0242 602398.

The museum is part of the Hailes Abbey ruins (chapter 5). It contains material recovered from the site, such as exquisitely carved stone fragments which may include some from the shrine of the 'holy blood'. Broken pieces of a stone knight effigy could be of Edmund, Earl of Cornwall (died 1300), or his brother Richard de Cornwall, who was killed at the Battle of Berwick in 1296. On a grander scale, there is an impressive display of vaulting bosses. Medieval titles include the Southam tile pavement and sixteen-tile 'Chertsey tile'. Pottery and clay pipes are among the post-dissolution exhibits. Outside, an enclosed area displays large pieces of carved stonework from various parts of the abbey, such as for vaulting or windows. They are mostly locally quarried freestones, but some are blue lias limestone from an unknown source.

LYDNEY
Lydney Park Museum, Lydney. Telephone: 0594 842844.

The museum, open for a limited season only, is in two rooms of the house at Lydney Park. The first contains excavated material from the nearby Roman temple of Nodens (chapter 3). This includes a lead curse, votive offerings of bronze rings and bone pins, spoons and brooches. Among small representations of dogs, a bronze wolfhound known as the 'Lydney Dog' is famous as a very fine piece of Romano-British sculpture. A penknife handle which depicts a dog chasing a hare was found in 1981. In contrast, the New Zealand Room contains many beautiful Maori objects collected by Viscount Bledisloe when he was Governor-General of New Zealand in the early twentieth century.

MORETON-IN-MARSH
Wellington Aviation Museum and Art Gallery, British School House, Broadway Road, Moreton-in-Marsh GL56 0BG. Telephone: 0608 50323.

This unique collection of Second World War aircraft paintings and fine art prints also has a small display on the history of the Wellington aeroplane. Striking objects on show include a sectioned Hercules radial engine, propellers and the tailplane of a Wellington from RAF Lossiemouth which crashed near Braemar in 1940. Profits from all sales are donated to the Royal Air Forces Benevolent Fund.

NEWENT
Shambles Museum of Victorian Life, 16-20 Church Street, Newent GL18 1PP. Telephone: 0531 822144.

This museum of Victorian family and commercial life in the Shambles of Newent incorporates a cobbled square and street with shops and workshops displaying merchandise, tools and utensils of the period. The four storeys of an eighteenth-century house have been furnished as a late Victorian tradesman's house.

NORTHLEACH
Cotswold Countryside Collection, Fosseway, Northleach GL54 3JH. Telephone: 0451 60715.

The museum contains the Lloyd-Baker Collection of Cotswold agricultural implements of the 1880s to 1920s, when horses were still the prime source of power. A special feature is an exhibition of Gloucestershire harvest wagons. There are also reconstructed blacksmith and wheelwright workshops. A gallery explains the social history of the Cotswolds from prehistoric to modern times. Special exhibitions and events on country themes

The Cotswold Countryside Collection at the old House of Correction, Northleach.

are arranged each year. The museum is in the former Northleach House of Correction, a 'country prison' of 1791. It was designed by Sir William Blackburn along the lines proposed by Sir George Onesiphorus Paul. Original cells can be viewed, as well as the courtroom which was in use from 1859 until 1974.

Keith Harding's World of Mechanical Music, High Street, Northleach GL54 3EU. Telephone: 0451 60181.

This is a fascinating collection of antique clocks, musical boxes, automata and mechanical musical instruments. Many of the machines are played during regular tours. Clocks and musical boxes are restored here and antique and other musical gifts are on sale.

OAKRIDGE
Oakridge Village Museum, Oakridge Lynch, near Bisley. Telephone: 028576 438.

The Oakridge Society keeps a room at the Methodist church containing a small collection of agricultural implements, old photographs of the Thames and Severn Canal, material on local worthies and other items of local interest. The museum has a limited opening.

SOUDLEY
Dean Heritage Centre, Camp Mill, Soudley, near Cinderford GL14 7UG. Telephone: 0594 822170.

This is the museum of the Forest of Dean, covering many aspects such as forestry, milling, coal mining and iron working. In addition, the Dean Heritage Museum Trust owns the Whitecliff Furnace near Coleford and the New Inn at Bream. For a fuller description see chapter 7.

STROUD
Stroud District (Cowle) Museum, Lansdown, Stroud GL5 1BB. Telephone: 0453 763394.

The museum's local geology collection includes minerals, fossils and mammoth teeth and tusks. A scale model of a dinosaur is set on one wall. Among the archaeological material are palaeolithic hand axes, iron age Armorican coins, Roman stone altars and a round stone burial cist with a heavy stone cover. The Folk Room contains musical instruments, glassware, traditional Gloucestershire pottery and a curious rocking bath. Two locally made lawnmowers, of about 1830 and 1860, are believed to be the second and third

oldest in the world.

Just across the road, Lansdown Hall contains the museum's Industrial Display, with items relating to the area's textile industry (including an 1890s hand-loom, a cross-cutter for finishing cloth and a braiding machine), brewing and coopering, dairying, ropemaking and walking-stick manufacturing, an industry which employed two thousand people in the Nailsworth and Chalford valleys in the 1870s. The restored clock from Dunkirk Mill (chapter 7) is among turret and other local clocks on show.

TETBURY
Tetbury Police Bygones Museum, The Old Court House, 63 Long Street, Tetbury GL8 8AA. Telephone: 0666 503552 or 504670.

At the very end of Long Street, the Old Police Station and Court House now house the tourist information centre and this museum. The cells of the old police station contain the exhibition, which has many items on loan from the Gloucestershire Constabulary.

TEWKESBURY
John Moore Countryside Museum, Church Street, Tewkesbury GL20 5SN. Telephone: 0684 297174.

The museum is in a timber-framed house which dates from about 1450. Displays commemorate the work of the local naturalist and writer John Moore and show man's impact on the countryside and the work of conservationists such as the Gloucestershire Trust for Nature Conservation.

The Little Museum, 45 Church Street, Tewkesbury. Telephone: 0684 297174.

This timber-framed house is part of the same row as the John Moore Museum and was restored in 1971. It shows a medieval merchant's shop and house and has been furnished with copies of period furniture.

Tewkesbury Town Museum, 64 Barton Street, Tewkesbury GL20 5PX. Telephone: 0684 295027.

The museum is in an early seventeenth-century timber-framed building which also houses the tourist information office. Exhibits include a carpenter's shop with two treadle lathes and other tools, a fine set of the borough's weights and measures of 1824, and displays concerning the Mop Fair, flooding of the Severn Vale, and Tewkesbury's architecture. Archaeological material includes Roman and medieval finds, and a large model shows the Battle of Tewkesbury in 1471.

TWIGWORTH
Nature in Art (The International Centre for Wildlife Art), Wallsworth Hall, Twigworth, Gloucester GL2 9PA. Telephone: 0452 731422.

Just off the A38 north of Gloucester, in the late eighteenth-century Wallsworth Hall, this museum is managed by the Society for Wildlife Art of the Nations. It is a wildlife art collection from all periods and countries, depicting all aspects of nature in many media including painting, pottery, glassware, mosaic and sculpture. There is also a programme of artists in residence, a gallery shop and a licensed coffee shop. Outside, there are sculptures, a nature garden, a pond and a children's play area.

WINCHCOMBE
Winchcombe Museum, Old Town Hall, High Street, Winchcombe GL54 5LJ. Telephone: 0242 602925.

The small folk museum has some bones from Belas Knap chambered tomb (chapter 3), neolithic flints and mosaic fragments from the Roman villa at Spoonley. A large toll board from the Winchcombe Turnpike Trust is hung on one wall. There is also a portrait of Jack of Newbury, a rich wool merchant who was born as John Smallwood at Winchcombe in the late fifteenth century. Much of the museum contains the Simms International Police Collection, with uniforms from all over the world. Smaller items include truncheons and helmets from different constabularies. Note also the stocks outside the Town Hall, as they have seven holes!

Winchcombe Railway Museum and Garden, 23 Gloucester Street, Winchcombe GL54 5LX. Telephone: 0242 602257 or 620641.

The museum has an outstanding collection of cast iron notices from many railway companies throughout Britain. There is a booking office and exhibits in the garden include signals and signal-box equipment which can be worked by visitors. The garden itself contains a Victorian vegetable garden and a medieval garden of medicinal herbs. Of related interest, the Gloucestershire-Warwickshire Railway is just north-east, at Toddington (chapter 8).

WOTTON-UNDER-EDGE
Wotton-under-Edge Historical Society Library and Museum, Public Library, Ludgate Hill, Wotton-under-Edge.

This is an archive of books, documents, maps, photographs and other items relating to Wotton-under-Edge and its vicinity.

Nature in Art (The International Centre for Wildlife Art), Wallsworth Hall, Twigworth.

The old coal dock at Bullo Pill.

7
Industrial archaeology

Despite its mainly rural character, Gloucester-shire has an industrial past of some importance. Many sites are connected with water transport, railways, textiles, quarrying or the iron and coal industries of the Forest of Dean. This district also has the famous miner's brass in Newland church (chapter 4) and the miners' tools inscribed on the font and tower of Abenhall church near Mitcheldean. A selection of sites is given here, with some grid references to locate smaller or less obvious sites. All can be seen from public roads or footpaths, but permission should be sought before entering private property.

Abbey Mill, Mill Street, Tewkesbury.

Now a restaurant, this corn-mill building of 1793 replaced an earlier one on the watercourse known as the Mill Avon. The abbey possessed a mill here by 1291, and probably earlier. There were finally five waterwheels, before milling declined after the opening of the Borough Mills in 1885. These impressive roller mills (Allied Mills) can be seen further upstream at the end of Quay Street.

Arlington Mill, Bibury.

The corn mill is an impressive seventeenth-century building, heavily buttressed when steam power was installed in 1851. In the eighteenth century it was used for fulling the locally produced cloth. It became dilapidated but was restored after 1965 with machinery brought from North Cerney Mill. The mill houses the Cotswold Country Museum and Gallery (telephone: 028574 368), including craftsmen's workshops, domestic bygones and Arts and Crafts movement furniture, but the collection's future is uncertain.

Bullo Pill port, near Newnham (OS 162: SO 691099).

This river port, just downstream from Newnham on the Severn estuary, was an important exporter of coal from 1809 until 1926. The coal chutes have been removed but the dock, which had entrance lock gates into the river, can be seen. There is also a pond which stored water for sluicing the dock. The coal was brought from the Cinderford area by the Forest of Dean Tramroad.

Clearwell Caves, Clearwell, near Coleford GL16 8JR. Telephone: 0594 32535 or 823700.

Clearwell Caves are a natural limestone cave system filled with iron ore, which has been mined here for over 2500 years, since the iron age and Roman periods. The huge mining complex covers more than 600 acres (245 ha), containing thousands of caverns and many miles of passages. Visitors follow passageways through the workings into eight large caverns (known locally as churns), passing equipment and displays showing how iron has been mined through the ages. Miners' pick marks can be seen in many places and there are also natural cave features such as calcite flowstones. One of the largest caverns, Barbeque Churn, 100 feet (30 metres) down, can hold over 350 people at functions such as the annual candlelit Hallowe'en barbecue. At the surface the engine house contains several vintage engines, including a 1925 horizontal Crossley engine which drives a 1915 Ingersoll Rand compressor for powering pneumatic drills. There is a shop and a teashop in the Miner's Canteen. Caving trips to the deeper levels can be arranged.

Coombe Hill Canal, near Cheltenham.

A 2$^{1}/_{2}$ mile (4 km) broad canal from the Severn at Wainlode (SO 884826) to Coombe Hill was in use from 1797 until 1876. Its main function was to carry Midlands coal to Cheltenham, even though it ended 5 miles (8 km) short of the town centre. It is now overgrown but contains some water, and it is possible to walk along the whole length. Part is a nature reserve. At Wharf End (SO 886273) the brick and stone canal basin can still be seen, as can the cottages which were built for canal workers.

Dean Heritage Centre, Camp Mill, Soudley, Cinderford GL14 7UG. Telephone: 0594 822170.

The complex is a museum of the Forest of Dean (chapter 6). In the early nineteenth century a large foundry was established here by Samuel Hewlett, making castings for tramroads, mines and engineering. Examples of Hewlett's work on display include a striking beam engine which worked at Lightmoor Colliery for over a century. A large corn mill was built in 1876 but twelve years later it was converted into a leatherboard mill making shoe insoles and heel stiffeners. From 1911 until 1952, the site operated as a sawmill, powered by a water turbine and diesel engines. It then served as a piggery and finally as a scrapyard. It was purchased for a museum in 1981, and a single waterwheel has been placed in one of the wheelpits. The museum covers the long history of the Forest, its industries and people.

Donnington Brewery, Upper Swell, near Stow-on-the-Wold (OS 163: SP 173277).

Thomas Arkell's rural brewery dates from 1865 and incorporates buildings of an earlier corn mill. The brewery is still in production and the millpond supplies two waterwheels which are still used occasionally, although the main power is a diesel engine. The brewery site can be viewed from nearby lanes.

The Dean Heritage Centre.

Dunkirk Mill, Nailsworth (OS 162: SO 845005).

This large cloth and hosiery mill beside the A46, with stone buildings dating from 1790 to 1860, was powered by five large waterwheels and a beam engine. The house and chimney of the latter survive, while the three remaining waterwheels are to be preserved. The complex is being converted into flats. Nearer Nailsworth, the seventeenth-century **Egypt Mill** is now a restaurant. It has been a woollen, cloth, logwood and flour mill. The **Stroud Valleys Cycle Trail** runs this way, passing fifteen mills as it follows the course of the Stonehouse to Nailsworth branch railway of 1867-1966.

Ebley Mill, Westward Road, Ebley, Stroud.

This fine stone-built textile mill of 1818 has a later *chateau*-style tower block of 1865 designed by G. F. Bodley, the architect of Selsley church (chapter 4). There were once five waterwheels and a beam engine here, the latter introduced in 1862 by the Marling family. There were eight hundred employees in 1870 and the mill worked until 1981. The building has been saved by conversion into offices for the Stroud District Council.

Forest of Dean railways

The courses of many tramways, railways and their branches can be traced throughout the Forest of Dean, built to serve the coal and iron industries. The Forest of Dean Tramway was built in 1809 as a horse-drawn plateway and later converted to broad-gauge and then standard-gauge edge rails. It took coal from around Cinderford for shipment at Bullo Pill (see above) but was later connected to the Great Western Railway's South Wales line. It was closed in 1967, but Haie Tunnel at Lower Soudley (SO 666102) survives as among the first railway tunnels in the world. A plate rail cast at the Cinderford Iron Works is displayed at the iron mine at Clearwell Caves (see above). The Severn and Wye Railway and Canal Company of 1810 was originally a plateway between Lydney and Lydbrook. There were branches to Coleford and Cinderford and in its later years it incorporated the line over the Severn Railway Bridge of 1879 to Sharpness. Some of its branches were never converted to standard gauge and, for example, the stone sleeper blocks of the plateway at Cannop Bicslade can still be seen in a valley at SO 605101. The Monmouth Tramway was laid in 1812 from Coleford and had a short branch to a tinplate works at Redbrook on the Wye, where an incline and bridge at SO 537103 still cross the B4231 on the county border with Gwent. The Forest of Dean Central Railway (1856-1961) to New Fancy Pit can be seen alongside the B4431 north-west from Blakeney. The Great Western Railway Museum at Coleford and Dean Forest Railway near Lydney are described in chapters 6 and 8.

Gloucester and Sharpness Canal

A ship canal from Berkeley Pill was conceived in 1784 as a means of avoiding the winding tidal Severn channel to Gloucester, but it was not until 1827 that a shorter 16 mile (26 km) canal was opened from Sharpness (SO 668022), where the Old Dock had a tidal basin and lock to the Severn. The New Dock was built in 1874 and is still busy with shipping of up to 5000 tons. A cut beneath a swing-

Forest of Dean railways: the incline at Redbrook.

Gloucester and Sharpness Canal: the bridge-keeper's cottage at Frampton-on-Severn.

bridge connects the dock with the canal, which is now used by pleasure craft to Gloucester. The large stone pier of another swing-bridge still stands beside the towpath a little way along the canal. This was a section of the Severn Railway Bridge of 1879, which was demolished exactly ninety years later, having been struck by a ship in the river. The canal has no locks but thirteen swing-bridges and several notable bridge-keepers' houses with Doric columns, such as for example at the Splatt and Saul bridges at Frampton-on-Severn (SO 743067 and 746085). The junction with the Stroudwater Canal can be seen near Saul at SO 757093.

Gloucester Docks

Gloucester's original port was alongside the tidal Severn, remembered by the road named The Quay, where the eighteenth-century custom house is now put to other use. The docks at the end of the ship canal were an entrepot or transhipment point between sea-going ships of up to 800 tons and river craft which continued up the Severn Navigation to Worcester, Stourport and beyond. There was much traffic in corn. Brick warehouses were built around the docks for storing goods in the late 1820s. Since the docks closed to commercial traffic the area has become a tourist attraction, with the conversion of the magnificent warehouses

to, for example, the National Waterways Museum, the Museum of Advertising and Packaging (chapter 6), the Gloucester Antiques Centre, offices and restaurants. In among all this is the stone Mariners' Church. There is a river lock to the Severn for navigation upstream by small vessels.

Leckhampton Quarries, Leckhampton Hill, Cheltenham.

Very extensive quarrying took place here, producing stone for the towns of Cheltenham and Gloucester in the vale below. There were tramways with stone sleeper blocks and inclined planes, some of which can be seen. The Devil's Chimney (SO 947184) is a local landmark left behind by the quarrymen (chapter 2). Some quarry faces remain open while others are overgrown all along the steep Cotswold scarp.

Lightmoor Colliery, Ruspidge, near Cinderford.

The site of this coal mine is just off the B4226, 1½ miles (2 km) south-west of Cinderford. It is now a timber yard, but it is possible to view a substantial stone beam-engine house still with its roof timbers (SO 641121). Other mine and railway buildings can be seen around the yard. Mine spoil tips stand in the forest, with the largest to the south-

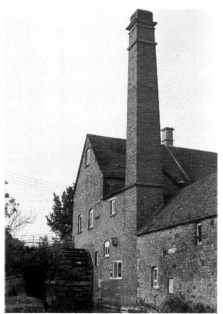

Lower Slaughter Mill.

east. A winding engine from this mine is preserved at the Dean Heritage Centre.

Lower Slaughter Mill, Lower Slaughter, near Bourton-on-the-Water.

The mill is a prominent feature at the top end of this pretty Cotswold village on the river Eye. The large iron waterwheel which can be seen outside the brick mill no longer works machinery, and a tall chimney shows that steam power was also employed here.

Lydney Harbour and Canal, Lydney.

This was the main port for the Forest of Dean's coal exports. The Lydney and Lydbrook Tramroad was connected to a new canal (1813) and tidal basin (1821) from the Severn. The harbour (SO 650014 to 635017) is now used by pleasure craft, but part of an old coal chute survives. The water in the dock is 24 feet (7.3 metres) above the sill of the sea lock. The entrance pier is a good place to view the lower Severn estuary, across to Sharpness Docks and down to the Severn road bridge. Near the railway station at the top end of the harbour, the striking Cookson Terrace (SO 635018) was built in 1858 for workers on the

Severn and Wye Railway. It is difficult to believe that there were shipyards near Lydney church in the seventeenth century when the Severn flowed further north than today.

New Mill, Kingswood, near Wotton-under-Edge (OS 162: ST 737930).

A five-storey textile mill in brick with a central clock-tower stands in a rural setting beside a large millpond. It has been put to other uses but can be seen from the B4058, a mile (1.6 km) west of Wotton-under-Edge. Also of interest, on the road nearby at ST 742930, is the round Bushford bridge tollhouse, with Gothic windows and crenellations.

Over Bridge, near Gloucester (OS 162: SO 816196).

This graceful stone-arched bridge of 1829 was designed by Thomas Telford, who was inspired by the Neuilly bridge built across the Seine by Perronet in 1768. It has a span of 150 feet (45.7 metres) over the Severn just outside Gloucester and now stands alone beside the dual carriageway of the A40, which bypassed it in 1974. Telford also designed the iron Mythe Bridge (1826) across the Severn further upstream at SO 889337 near Tewkesbury, which carries the A438 into Hereford.

Parkend blowing-engine house, Parkend, Forest of Dean (OS 162: SO 616079).

This tall house contained a beam engine for blowing air at a blast-furnace. It has since been converted to a dwelling and is now a field study centre which can be seen beside the B4234 in Parkend village.

St Mary's Mill, Chalford, near Stroud (OS 162: SO 886022).

This mill can be seen from the A419 across the railway line and canal which follow the natural routeway through the Golden Valley south-east of Stroud. On the site of an earlier fulling mill, it was rebuilt in 1820 as a textile mill, later becoming a paper mill and flock mill. From 1903 until 1981 it was used for manufacturing walking sticks, an important industry in the Stroud district. A waterwheel and steam engine have survived here.

Shapridge Guns Mills charcoal furnace, near Littledean (OS 162: SO 675159).

What is said to be the finest example of a charcoal blast-furnace in England can be seen from a lane in a valley bottom 1½ miles (2 km)

St Mary's Mill with the railway and the canal in the foreground.

north-north-east of Littledean. This early seventeenth-century furnace worked during the Civil War to produce ammunition, and dates cast on the iron lintels show it was rebuilt in 1682-3. It closed in 1743 when the site became a paper mill. The bellows room and wheelpit survive next to the furnace tower, upon which now stands a remarkable timber-framed building.

Stanley Mill, Ryeford, near Stroud (OS 162: SO 813043).

This is a large brick-built mill of five floors. It was an early fireproof mill when rebuilt in 1812-13, with the floors supported by iron arches on cast iron columns. Power came from five waterwheels and a beam engine of 1820. The mill building and mill lodge can be seen from the road to Kings Stanley.

Stanley Mill.

55

Stroudwater Canal, Framilode to Wallbridge, Stroud.

Opened in 1779 to bring coal to the textile mills in the Stroud valley, this canal had thirteen locks in its 8 mile (13 km) length from the Severn at Framilode (SO 751105) and the canal could take trows up to 72 feet (22 metres) long. It was closed to navigation in 1941. The junction with the Gloucester and Sharpness Canal can be seen at Saul (SO 757093). The stone-built company offices survive at Bath Road in Stroud (SO 846051), at the Wallbridge terminus from which the Thames and Severn Canal continues east. The canal is under restoration by the Stroudwater, Thames and Severn Canal Trust.

Thames and Severn Canal, Wallbridge to Inglesham.

This was a 29 mile (46 km) canal opened in 1789 from the Stroudwater Canal at Wallbridge (SO 846051) to Inglesham (SU 204988) on the Thames near Lechlade. Its function was to link the two important navigable English rivers, and the watershed between them was breached by the greatest engineering work on the canal, the Sapperton Tunnel. It took $5^{1}/2$ years to complete its $2^{1}/4$ mile (3.6 km) length. It was the longest canal tunnel of its day and is still the third longest in Britain. Its interior collapsed after this section of the canal closed in 1927. At the east end, the classical-styled Coates portal (SO 965006) was restored in 1976-7. The Daneway portal is at Sapperton (SO 944033). At each end, the Tunnel House Inn and Daneway Inn were built for the benefit of the tunnellers. The last section to work, from Stroud to Chalford, was closed in 1933. The Stroudwater, Thames and Severn Canal Trust aims to restore the canal. The towpath can be followed from Wallbridge to Sapperton. The canal company built conspicuous round tower houses for the workers, such as can be seen at Inglesham (SU 204988) or Chalford (SO 892025).

Whitecliff Furnace, near Coleford (OS 162: SO 568103).

This impressive blast-furnace over 30 feet (9 metres) high, was one of the first in Dean to use coke fuel for iron smelting at the start of the nineteenth century (it has a datestone of 1806). It is undergoing excavation and restoration by the Dean Heritage Museum Trust and, although there is no admission to the public, it can be seen from the lane to Newland just half a mile (0.8 km) south-west of Coleford. It is complemented by the earlier charcoal furnace at Shapridge (see above).

Left: *Thames and Severn Canal: the Coates portal of the Sapperton Tunnel.*
Right: *Whitecliff Furnace near Coleford.*

Cotswold sheep at the Cotswold Farm Park.

8
Other places to visit

Bibury Trout Farm, Bibury, near Cirencester GL7 5NL. Telephone: 028574 215.

At this large working fish farm in the centre of Bibury rainbow trout are hatched and reared. Visitors can relax in the water gardens, picnic, feed the trout or even try fishing (tackle supplied). There is a shop for the purchase of trout and other gifts.

Birdland, Rissington Road, Bourton-on-the-Water GL54 2BN. Telephone: 0451 20689.

The bird gardens are in an idyllic setting beside a stream. As well as ducks, geese and swans, other birds are at liberty, such as macaws, parrots, cockatoos and lorikeets. The largest collection of penguins outside America can be seen in a glass-sided pool. Birdland is concerned with conservation and various birds are bred here.

Cotswold Farm Park, Guiting Power, near Cheltenham GL54 5NA. Telephone: 0451 850307.

This is a large and important collection of rare breeds of British farm animals, which admirably shows the work of the Rare Breeds Survival Trust. These include the tiny Soay sheep, the Cotswold Lions sheep, Old Gloucester cattle, Gloucester Old Spot pigs and iron age pigs. There are farm nature trails around this high Cotswold farm. Attractions for children include a pets corner and an adventure playground. There is a picnic area and refreshments are also available. Seasonal under-cover exhibits include lambing and shearing.

Cotswold Water Park, Somerford Keynes, South Cerney and Fairford. Telephone: 0285 861459.

The main park is spread over a very extensive area of nearly one hundred flooded gravel pits in the upper Thames valley around Somerford Keynes and South Cerney, with part also in Wiltshire. Here are the Keynes and Neigh Bridge Country Parks and the Somerford Lakes Reserve. There are facilities for angling, sailing, windsurfing and water-skiing, and also birdwatching in several nature reserves. The second, smaller part of the water park is in the lower Coln valley between Fairford and Lechlade.

The Gloucestershire-Warwickshire Railway at Toddington station.

Dean Forest Railway, Norchard Steam Centre, near Lydney. Telephone: 0594 843423.

The headquarters of the Dean Forest Railway is the Norchard Steam Centre, situated in a valley beside the B4234 road northwards from Lydney to Parkend. There are train rides on steam days, but there is always a permanent static display of railway locomotives, coaches and wagons, as well as a museum. There is also a gift shop and picnic area.

Donnington Fish Farm, Condicote Lane, near Upper Swell, Stow-on-the-Wold GL54 1EP. Telephone: 0451 30873.

Rainbow trout are reared at this fish farm, which is based in an eighteenth-century stone barn. Visitors can feed the larger fish and there are facilities for fly-fishing in a small secluded lake. The farm shop sells a variety of trout products.

Folly Farm Waterfowl, Duckpool Valley, near Bourton-on-the-Water GL54 3BY. Telephone: 0451 20285.

Here in the attractive Duckpool Valley is a leading conservation centre for over 150 rare breeds of domestic ducks, geese, chickens and wildfowl. Friendly hand-reared rabbits, goats and deer are popular with children. Folly Farm also has a garden centre, tea room and camping and caravan site.

The Glassbarn, 31 Culver Street, Newent GL18 1DB. Telephone: 0531 821173.

Visitors can see workers at this glass-blowing workshop using traditional methods to produce hand-made glassware with contemporary designs noted for their use of colour. Products can be purchased in the showroom and shop.

Gloucestershire-Warwickshire Railway, Toddington Station, Toddington, Cheltenham GL54 5DT. Telephone: 0242 621405.

Steam passenger trains work along 4 miles (6 km) of restored railway track from the old railway station at Toddington to Winchcombe and Gretton Meadow. This is part of the old Honeybourne line from Cheltenham to Stratford-upon-Avon, which closed in 1976. The eventual aim is to re-open the line to Cheltenham racecourse and then northwards to Broadway and Honeybourne. Facilities at Toddington station include a shop and cafeteria, while steam locomotives can be seen under restoration in the yard.

Gloucester Ski Centre, Robinswood Hill, Gloucester GL4 9EA. Telephone: 0452 414300.

The two long dry-ski slopes with three ski-lifts are prominent features on the east side of Robinswood Hill, close to Gloucester. The centre is available for beginners (by appointment) and experts, with tuition available. Equipment can be hired and there is also a ski shop.

Model Railway Exhibition, Box Bush, High Street, Bourton-on-the-Water. Telephone: 0451 20686.

The exhibition has around 400 square feet (37 square metres) of model layouts, with over forty British and continental trains in 00/H0 and N gauges. There is also a shop selling models and accessories.

Model Village, The Old New Inn, High Street, Bourton-on-the-Water GL54 2AF. Telephone: 0451 20467.

This is an excellent model at one-ninth scale of Bourton-on-the-Water, with the walls and roofs of the houses authentically built in local stone, complete with cottage gardens and the river Windrush. The model village was first opened in 1937 and finished three years later.

At the National Birds of Prey Centre, Newent.

National Birds of Prey Centre, Newent GL18 1JJ. Telephone: 0531 820286.

There are over sixty species of birds of prey here. Trained eagles, falcons, owls and vultures can be seen in flying demonstrations, while other birds can be seen nesting and rearing their young in the aviaries. Refreshments, a gift shop and picnic area are available at the centre, which is also known as the Falconry Centre and is 1 mile (1.6 km) south-west of Newent.

Newent Butterfly and Natural World Centre, Springbank, Birches Lane, Newent GL18 1DN. Telephone: 0531 821800.

The centre features tropical butterflies flying free in a jungle-type garden of exotic plants, a large live insect gallery, a collection of snakes and lizards, natural history and water life exhibitions, rare breeds of poultry, fancy pheasants, waterfowl and aviaries of other birds.

Prinknash Bird Park, Prinknash Park, Cranham, Gloucester GL4 8EX. Telephone: 0452 812727.

Situated below Prinknash Abbey and Pottery are 9 acres (3.6 ha) of attractive parkland and lakes, containing waterfowl, peacocks, exotic pheasants, tame deer and pygmy goats.

Prinknash Pottery, Prinknash Abbey, Cranham, Gloucester GL4 8EX. Telephone: 0452 812239.

The Benedictine community welcomes visitors to their abbey (chapter 4) and pottery, which command breathtaking views over the Severn Vale. There are guided tours of the Pottery Viewing Gallery and most of the articles made in the pottery are on sale in the gift shop, along with many other items.

Puzzle Wood, near Coleford. Telephone: 0594 33187.

This fascinating area of ancient Roman iron workings was landscaped in the nineteenth century. There are scenic walks through the trees, with paths arranged in a puzzle with steps and bridges. There is a tea garden and souvenir shop.

Selsley Herb and Goat Farm, Water Lane, Selsley, near Stroud. Telephone: 0453 766682.

This formal herb garden has over 150 varieties of herbs. The farm also has friendly goats and a shop.

Three Choirs Vineyards, Rhyle House, Welsh House Lane, Newent GL18 1LR. Telephone: 053185 223 or 555.

The vineyard, which now covers over 42 acres (17 ha), was planted in 1973 and began producing quality English wines two years later. Visitors can walk around the vineyard (a map is provided) or conducted tours of the vineyard and winery can be arranged for parties.

Wildfowl and Wetlands Centre, Slimbridge, Cambridge, Gloucester GL2 7BT. Telephone: 0453 890065.

Slimbridge is the headquarters of the Wildfowl and Wetlands Trust. The centre was established by the late Sir Peter Scott and its 800 acres (324 ha) contain the greatest collection of waterfowl in the world. Many live here permanently, including varieties of flamingoes. Hides look over the saltmarshes of the Severn estuary, which is the winter home of many birds such as white-fronted geese. There are information boards and facilities for disabled visitors, an exhibition area, restaurant, shop and other facilities. Slimbridge is easily located, for the tall spire of the village church is a conspicuous landmark in the flat Vale of Berkeley.

Winchcombe Pottery, Winchcombe, Cheltenham GL54 5NU. Telephone; 0242 602462.

The pottery is situated 1 mile (1.6 km) north of Winchcombe, just off the Broadway Road (B4632). It was established in 1926 on the site of an early nineteenth-century pottery. The pottery now produces a wide range of hand-thrown stoneware pots for use in the home, fired to 1300° C in a wood-fired kiln. Visitors can look around the showroom and at most times the workshop. A furniture maker, sculptor, decorative painter and upholsterer also work on the premises.

The Wildfowl and Wetlands Centre, with the bust of Sir Peter Scott, its founder.

Lower Slaughter.

9
Towns and villages

BERKELEY
Early closing Wednesday

Dominated by its castle (chapter 5) and nuclear power station, this small town is not without interest. It is known to have been of some importance in Saxon times but today the streets are lined with mostly brick houses and inns of the eighteenth and nineteenth centuries. The stone-built town hall stands at one end of the Market Place and there is a shop dated 1666 at the corner of High Street. Just off the street the Jenner Museum (chapter 6) is in the former home of Edward Jenner, the pioneer of smallpox vaccination. Close by the castle, the tall church (St Mary) has some Norman work but is mainly of the thirteenth and fifteenth centuries. Wall decorations include a Doom painting above the high chancel arch. Among the Berkeley family monuments are the effigies of Thomas, Lord Berkeley at the time of Edward II's murder, and his second wife, Lady Katherine. The grave of Edward Jenner is in the chancel. The bell-tower of 1753 is separate, standing just to the north across the churchyard of table-top tombs. The Little Avon river enters the Severn estuary at Berkeley Pill, which was a trading port from medieval times to the nineteenth century, when sailing barges (trows) came here. Today, **Sharpness** is a busy port on the Severn and at the start of the Gloucester and Sharpness Canal (chapter 7). 1 1/2 miles (2 km) west of Berkeley, the world's first commercial nuclear power station supplied electricity from 1962 until 1989, when it was shut down for decommissioning.

BIBURY

William Morris called Bibury 'the most beautiful village in England'. It has since become a popular tourist spot, in the valley of the river Coln, which flows through its centre. At the east end is the church, which dates back to Saxon times and contains Norman and Early English work and some notable tombs. Nearby, Bibury Court (now an hotel) has a wing of 1639 said to have been designed by Inigo Jones. On the west side of the river is **Arlington**, where can be seen the famous picturesque row of early seventeenth-century cottages (National Trust). There is a pleasant walk away from the traffic beside a stream to Arlington

The double lock-up at Bisley.   *The Bear Inn, Bisley.*

Mill (chapter 7). The Bibury Trout Farm here was one of the first to be established in Britain (chapter 8). Further upstream, the small hamlet of **Ablington** escapes the bustle of Bibury.

BISLEY

Bisley is a high Cotswold village of some charm, formerly important for weaving. The church (All Saints) has a spire and contains a carved font with two fish inside the bowl and a shepherd and sheep on the base. In the churchyard is the curious Poor Soul's Light, a stone wellhead beneath a spire which once held candles for masses for the poor. Below the church are the Seven Springs, which are blessed and decorated with flowers on Ascension Day. At the top of the village, near the Bear Inn, is the well preserved lock-up of 1824 with two cells beneath an ogee gable. Beside the Stroud road, 1 mile (1.6 km) north-west, are the base and shaft of a Saxon cross, carved with holy figures, while nearby is Lypiatt Park, where the Gunpowder Plot conspirators are said to have held a meeting. To the south, there is a small local museum at Oakridge Lynch (chapter 6).

BLOCKLEY

This hillside village has some interesting architecture. Six silk mills were a major source of employment here by 1880, shortly before this industry collapsed. There are attractive terraced weavers' cottages at Northend,

the top end of the village, with humbler nineteenth-century examples further on. The church is spacious and has work dating back to the Norman period. The tower, however, is eighteenth-century. To the north, Northwick Park is an early seventeenth-century house remodelled in about 1685, the 1730s and the early nineteenth century. It has been converted into flats.

BOURTON-ON-THE-WATER
Early closing Saturday

This is an extremely popular Cotswold village, with five low bridges crossing the river Windrush as it flows past the Green and High Street. At the top end of the High Street, the eighteenth-century church tower is recognisable for its small dome on top. Inside, the chancel dates from 1328 but much of the church has been restored. Upstream, next to the Broad Bridge of 1756, the old mill has been turned into the Cotswolds Motor Museum (chapter 6), while further down the High Street other attractions are the Model Railway Exhibition and the Model Village, with Birdland off Rissington Road (chapter 8). The village extends to the west side of the river, where a pottery and perfumery are open to visitors. Among special events held in the village, six-a-side football is played in the Windrush on August Bank Holiday Mondays. Bourton can claim early origins. The iron age Salmonsbury Camp was just north-east of the town centre, where a hoard of 147 currency bars was found in 1860. There was later a Roman settlement, and it is said that the church is on the site of a Roman temple.

BREAM

Bream is a mainly new village, although the New Inn here dates from around 1500. Even earlier are the Scowles and Devil's Chapel, now overgrown but ancient open-cast iron workings of at least Roman date. The impressive grey stone war memorial stands at a high point on the west side of the village and looks out over an expanse of woodland, for Bream is one of the gateways to the Forest of Dean.

CHALFORD

Very steep narrow lanes and weavers' cottages are prominent features of this village on the south-facing side of the Golden Valley, 3 miles (5 km) from Stroud. Important road, rail and canal routes follow the valley bottom, where there are eighteenth-century mills. Here is also the church, built in 1724 but altered in the following century. A memorial to Richard Selby Thomas was carved by John Thomas, who worked on statues for the Houses of Parliament. Just below the church is the old Thames and Severn Canal (chapter 7) and a round house, still inhabited, which was built for canal workers. Below this, again are the Belvedere Mill and its millpond.

CHELTENHAM
Early closing Wednesday and Saturday; market days Tuesday to Saturday.

A mineral spring at the foot of the Cotswold scarp was discovered in 1715, and this led to a small village being transformed into one of the great Regency spa towns of Europe. The first pump room was built in 1738 and the full spa was established fifty years later when King George III stayed at Bayshill Lodge. A new town was laid out in 1800-40, with wide streets and tree-lined squares designed mostly by J. B. Papworth. The town has spread to envelop the old settlements of **Charlton Kings** and **Leckhampton.**

The Promenade is the principal shopping street with large department stores, although the main terrace (about 1823) contains the municipal offices. In front are war memorials and a statue of Dr Edward Wilson sculpted by Captain Scott's widow two years after Wilson perished with her husband in the Antarctic in 1912. Opposite are the Imperial Gardens, with the Town Hall (1901) at one end and the Jearrad brothers' imposing Queen's Hotel (1838) at the other. Beyond, shops in the unusual Montpellier Walk are separated by caryatids or female statues. At the end is the Rotunda, with its dome of 1825 by Papworth based on the Pantheon in Rome. This was the Montpellier Spa but is now a branch of Lloyd's Bank. The interior is spectacular and the foyer displays the eighteenth-century Italian marble

The Royal Crescent, Cheltenham.

Montpellier Walk, Cheltenham.

Napoleon Fountain. Across the road, Montpellier Park is pleasant with mature trees. Number 91 Montpellier Terrace was the birthplace in 1872 of Dr Wilson of Antarctic fame. The convex curve of Lansdown Crescent was designed in about 1830 by Papworth and the Jearrads. The town is noted for its educational establishments. In Bath Road, the Cheltenham College was opened in 1843 for the sons of Indian Army officers. It was designed by J. Wilson in a Gothic style and now includes the classical Thirlstane House. The Cheltenham Ladies' College was founded in 1854, but the austere buildings facing Montpellier Street and St George's Road date from 1873. Miss Dorothea Beale, a pioneer of women's education, was principal after 1858.

The concave Royal Crescent of 1806 is the oldest in the town but is rather marred by facing the bus station. The Art Gallery and Museum (chapter 6) is in Clarence Street. Nearby, the parish church (St Mary) dates back to the twelfth and fourteenth centuries but was restored in the nineteenth century. Its dark interior is due to the stained glass, of which the rose window in the north transept is of note. Outside is the shaft of a fourteenth-century preaching cross. Further north in Portland Street is Holy Trinity church of 1820-3, designed by G. A. Underwood and containing memorials to retired officials from India. The composer Gustav Holst was born on 21st September 1874 at Number 4 Clarence Road,

where the house is now a museum (chapter 6). Across the road is the Pittville Gate, entrance to a new spa district established by Joseph Pitt, Member of Parliament and banker in the late Regency period. The domed and colonnaded Pittville Pump Room (chapter 6) was completed by J. B. Forbes in 1830. Set in parkland, it was to have been the centre of the estate, which was never fully completed. The Regency-style Clarence and Wellington Squares off West Drive were part of this ambitious development.

Cheltenham is noted for its festivals. In March there is the Cheltenham National Hunt Festival, held at the racecourse at Prestbury Park to the north of the town. Events include the famous Cheltenham Gold Cup steeplechase. The Cheltenham Music Festival has been held at the beginning of July every year since 1944, while the Festival of Literature takes place in October.

CHIPPING CAMPDEN
Early closing Thursday.

Perhaps the best of the Cotswolds wool towns, Chipping Campden's charter dates back to 1180. The attractive High Street is mainly of stone, although there are some half-timbered houses. In the middle stand the Victorian Town Hall and Market Hall (National Trust) of 1627 on stone pillars and arches. Grevel House has a fine two-storeyed bay window of about 1380. This was the home of William Grevel, who enriched the church and is said to be the source for the merchant in Chaucer's *Canterbury Tales*. Opposite is the Woolstaplers' Hall, built in about 1340 for Robert Calf. It was where the wool merchants traded and is now the museum (chapter 6) and tourist information centre. The curve of the High Street continues into Leysbourne, where there is the small Ernest Wilson Memorial Garden, dedicated to an important Victorian gardener and plant collector. The church (chapter 4) is clear evidence of the town's former wealth. Beside it are the lodges and arched gateway of the ruined Campden House, which was burnt down to prevent it falling into enemy hands in the Civil War. It was the home built by Sir Baptist Hicks, the first Lord Campden, a philanthropist and supporter of Charles I. In Church Street, he built the tall-chimneyed stone almshouses in 1612 for six poor men and six poor women. Opposite is a wheel wash for carriages and wagons. In the late spring, the Scuttlebrook Wake includes a fair in the High Street, while Robert Dover's Games are held on nearby Dover's Hill (chapter 2).

CINDERFORD

Cinderford was a coal-mining settlement in the heart of the Forest of Dean. The mines have now closed but their spoil tips can be glimpsed among the surrounding trees. The Baptist chapel of 1860 is of warehouse proportions.

CIRENCESTER

Early closing Thursday; market days Monday and Friday.

This thriving market town is the 'capital of the Cotswolds'. In Roman times it was *Corinium Dobunnorum*, the largest town outside London. The wool trade and abbey brought wealth in the middle ages. The former was responsible for the great church (chapter 4) which faces the Market Place, the scene of great activity on market days. Here there are stone houses of the seventeenth to nineteenth centuries with painted fronts, and the Corn Hall which houses the tourist information centre. Between Castle Street and Cricklade Street, part of the old town brewery has been converted to the Niccol Centre for the arts, while craftsmen can be seen working at the Cirencester Workshops. Along Cricklade

Street, the distinctive brewery maltings have become flats. Further south, the town lock-up (chapter 6) is worth finding in the grounds of the Cotswold District Offices in Trinity Road, while the Roman amphitheatre (chapter 3) is nearby across the ring road. The Abbey Grounds is a large park to the north of the Market Place. Nothing remains here of Cirencester Abbey except the late Norman Spital Gateway at the north end off the busy Grove Lane. Nearby are traces of the Roman town wall (chapter 3). In Spitalgate Street are almshouses and the preserved arcades of the chantry of St John's Hospital, founded in 1133 by Henry I. Returning to the Market Place, there are attractive wool merchants' houses in Dollar Street and Godsditch Street, and the Weavers' Hall in Thomas Street. Park Street has the Corinium Museum (chapter 6), where many excavated finds from the Roman town are displayed. Just west, Cirencester House is surrounded by high yew hedges, but Cirencester Park is open to the public and entered at Cecily Hill (chapter 5). Off the Fosse Way to the south-west is the Royal Agricultural College, a large Gothic-style mansion designed by Dankes.

CLEARWELL

This small village in a quiet valley on the edge of the Forest of Dean takes its name from

The Market Place, Cirencester.

The Market Hall, Dursley.

a spring of good water. There is a tall medieval cross in the centre, but the red sandstone church and spire are of the nineteenth century. Clearwell Castle, a Gothic-revival house built for the Wyndham family in 1727, is now a country house hotel. Nearby there are the ancient iron mines at Clearwell Caves and Puzzle Wood, both open to the public (chapters 7 and 8).

COLEFORD
Early closing Thursday.

Coleford is the 'capital of the Forest of Dean' and a good centre from which to explore it. The bell-tower of the church stands in the centre, near the town hall. It was built in 1821 on the site of an earlier chapel of ease to Newland, but when it was replaced by a new church all except the tower was demolished in 1882 to provide stone to build a boys' school. Bank Street has the headquarters of the Forestry Commission, in a handsome building built as a bank in 1786. The Deputy Governor for the Forest of Dean also has an office here. The Great Western Railway Museum (chapter 6) is in the car park off Railway Drive. Coleford is associated with ironworking, with the Whitecliff Furnace nearby and the mines at Clearwell Caves 1 1/2 miles (2 km) to the south (chapter 7). The pioneering ironfounder David Mushet lived here, where his son Robert was born in 1811. The latter is commemorated on a plaque at Mushet Place, on the site of the barn

where he improved the Bessemer process of manufacturing steel in 1856 and discovered self-hardening steel in 1868.

DURSLEY
Early closing Wednesday.

The town is situated in a valley overlooked by Cam Peak and Stinchcombe Hill. It became prosperous as a cloth-making centre, with mills later established further down at Cam, where one mill still operates. The eighteenth-century Market Hall stands on twelve arches at a busy junction in the town centre. It has a bell turret and a statue of Queen Anne facing the church. The church incorporates a chapel of the 1450s, believed to have been built by the merchant Thomas Tanner, and an early eighteenth-century tower. Long Street is the most attractive street hereabouts, with mainly eighteenth-century houses. At the bottom is the Priory, a large house built in 1539 for the Webbs, the name taken by a family of Flemish weavers who settled here and are said to have taught their craft to the people of Dursley. It is now offices for the adjacent Lister Petter factory. The firm of R. A. Lister and Company was established in 1867 and became famous for the manufacture of agricultural machinery and engines. The curving Castle Street takes its name from the vanished castle built in Norman times by Roger de Berkeley. Up the hill to the south-east, **Woodmancote** has good examples of Georgian houses, among the best buildings at Dursley. Further up the valley on the Stroud road, **Uley** was a weaving village, with seventeenth and eighteenth-century houses. It was famous for its blue broadcloth.

DYMOCK

This is a small village in the Vale of Leadon, in the north-west corner of the county near the border with Hereford and Worcester. Standing behind Wintour's Green is the long church of red sandstone with a sturdy tower supporting a squat spire. There are traces of Norman work in the walls, but the church was altered in the thirteenth and fourteenth centuries. Dymock is known for its poets. Lascelles Abercrombie lived here just before and during the First World War, and visitors who stayed for periods included Rupert Brooke, W. H. Davies, Robert Frost and Wilfrid Gibson.

EASTLEACH

Eastleach Turville and Eastleach Martin are

two small villages separated by the river Leach. Their churches both have Norman doorways and are most unusually sited almost facing each other across the river. A picturesque clapper bridge is known as Keble's Bridge after John Keble, who was curate here for eight years.

FAIRFORD

Fairford is on the river Coln near the south border of the county. The beautiful church (chapter 4) is famed for its medieval stained glass windows. Mill Lane leads north-west from the top of the High Street to a mill and bridge, from which there is a good view looking back to the church. Next to the churchyard, the free school of 1738 is now a library and youth centre. This is on the High Street, which is attractive with houses and shops as it descends to a square. In a house here the cleric and poet John Keble was born in 1792. Keble College, Oxford was founded in memory of this man, who was instrumental in reviving the established Church of England. The main road through Fairford is constricted by the narrows of Bridge Street and London Street, across which a path leads to a riverside walk. Part of the Cotswold Water Park (chapter 8) is in flooded gravel pits between Fairford and Lechlade. Just to the south, the large Royal Air Force base was the scene of early trial flights of Concorde. Its long main runway crosses into Wiltshire and back.

FRAMPTON-ON-SEVERN

This long village claims to have the largest green in England, in which two ponds and a cricket pitch are completely lost. Notable houses set back from the green include Frampton Court, a Georgian mansion with

gardens and a unique orangery, and the timbered Frampton Manor, with a fifteenth-century barn and dovecote. Both can be visited by prior arrangement. The church is at the far south end of the village, near Splatt Bridge and the Gloucester and Sharpness Canal (chapter 7). It has been restored but contains a rare Norman lead font.

GLOUCESTER

Early closing Wednesday; market day Saturday.

The capital city of Gloucestershire has had a distinguished history. It owes its origins to the Romans, who established a fort at the lowest crossing of the Severn towards Wales. The colonia *Glevum* followed soon after. In Anglo-Saxon times it was *Gleawcester*, one of King Alfred's fortified burhs with a royal mint. William the Conqueror decided to implement the Domesday Survey while staying here. The great abbey became the cathedral at the Dissolution. There was much destruction when the city withstood a Civil War siege in 1643. Gloucester was also a port, at first on the river Severn and then after 1827 with its own docks connected by a ship canal to Sharpness (chapter 7). Despite reconstruction and the building of modern shops, there is much to see around the city centre. The Roman plan survives in the main streets which meet at the Cross, where St Michael's Tower is a prominent feature and the tourist information centre. From here, Eastgate Street has the Renaissance-style Guildhall and the portico of the Eastgate Market, preserved and rebuilt in 1973. Beneath Boots's shop are displayed the remains of the Roman and medieval city wall and east gateway (see chapter 3). At street level, the signposted *via sacra* follows the old

The village green and orangery, Frampton-on-Severn.

Robert Raikes's house in Southgate Street, Gloucester.

city walls around Gloucester as closely as possible. Off Eastgate Street, Brunswick Road has the City Museum and Art Gallery (chapter 6).

In Northgate Street, the timbered New Inn was a pilgrim's hostelry of about 1450 and its galleried courtyard is an unexpected delight amongst modern shops. Across the road, St John's church is mainly early eighteenth-century, but its tower and truncated spire are fourteenth-century. The top of the spire stands in a small garden in Hare Lane, where there are two historic timber-framed buildings. The Raven Centre, wrongly known as the Raven Inn, dates from about 1520 and may have been the home of the Hoare family who emigrated to America. It was restored in 1949. Ye Olde Fish Shoppe is dated around 1535. Opposite is the Sainsbury's Mural, which tells the history of Gloucester from the iron age onwards.

There are several houses of interest in Westgate Street. The most hidden but most spectacular in Gloucester is behind the shop front of Number 26. A very narrow passage, once called Maverdine Lane, gives an unforgettable view of the four storeys of the timber-framed Judge's House. It was the town house of the Guise and Clifford families but is popularly known as the headquarters of Colonel Massey, who led the city's defence during the siege of 1643. In contrast, the classical Shire Hall (Gloucestershire County Council) was designed by Sir Robert Smirke in 1816. The

Folk Museum (chapter 6) is also called Bishop Hooper's Lodging, because he is said to have stayed here the night before being burnt at the stake in 1555. The reputed burnt stump of the stake is in the museum. Opposite is St Nicholas's church with a prominent truncated spire. Off Westgate Street, College Street leads to the cathedral, which towers over the city (chapter 4). Gloucester Cathedral shares the Three Choirs Festival with Hereford and Worcester, an event which dates from the early eighteenth century. In nearby College Court, the 'home' of Beatrix Potter's Taylor of Gloucester is now a museum and shop (chapter 6). In St Mary's Street, the thirteenth-century gateway into the former abbey precinct is faced by Bishop Hooper's Monument, erected on the site of his martyrdom. Behind is St Mary de Lode church.

In Southgate Street, the Old Bell Inn was the town house of the Berkeley family. Robert Raikes's House is an impressive timbered house of about 1560. This pioneer of the Sunday school movement is buried across the road in St Mary de Crypt church (chapter 4). The preacher George Whitefield attended St Mary de Crypt School, next to the church. Blackfriars is a well preserved Dominican friary off Ladybellegate Street (chapter 5). Southgate Street continues outside the old city to Bristol Road, where the Morelands Trading Estate factory building at the junction with Clifton Road recalls the manufacturing of the famous 'England's Glory' matches.

Since their closure to commercial shipping, Gloucester Docks (chapter 7) have become a major tourist attraction, with a unique dockscape of tall brick warehouses preserved by conversion to offices, restaurants, Antique Centre, National Waterways Museum and Museum of Advertising and Packaging (chapter 6). The Regiments of Gloucestershire Museum is in the Custom House (see chapter 6). Along the riverside to the north is St Bartholomew's Hospital, rebuilt as almshouses in Gothic style in 1789, while to the south are the ruins of Llanthony Priory (chapter 5).

GREAT and LITTLE BARRINGTON

Great Barrington is a large estate village on the north side of the Windrush, where Barrington Park is a Palladian mansion in a deer park. The church has a Norman chancel arch but is mostly of the fifteenth century. Memorials include one of 1620 showing Captain Edmund Bray wearing his sword on the wrong side, which he did in life since being pardoned for killing a man. The finest is a marble monument to the children Edward and Jane Bray who died of smallpox in 1711. Across the Windrush is Little Barrington, an attractive village of stone houses. This was the source of Barrington stone and there are the hollows and mounds of former quarry workings all around the village and at neighbouring Windrush.

LECHLADE

Lechlade is an important focus of land and water routeways, with two river crossings of the Thames or Isis close to the borders with Oxfordshire and Wiltshire. The old Salt Way leads away north-westwards, eventually to Droitwich. Freestone quarried at Taynton near Burford was loaded into barges at Lechlade and sent downstream for building St Paul's Cathedral. The Thames and Severn Canal (chapter 7) met the Thames here at the confluence of the Thames and Coln, where the Round House was built for canal workers. Halfpenny Bridge was once a tollbridge and takes the A361 out of Lechlade to the south, giving access to a park and riverside walk (actually in Wiltshire) downstream to St John's Bridge. Here are the highest lock on the navigable Thames and a Victorian statue of Father Thames which formerly stood at the head of

the Thames near Cirencester. In Lechlade itself there are attractive brick and stone houses and inns, centred on a square and a church with a slender spire, visible from afar. Features within St Lawrence's church of 1476 include the font, carved timber bosses in the chancel roof supported by stone corbels, the east window of about 1510, the brass of the wool merchant and benefactor John Townsend (died 1458) and a carved figure of St Agatha in the north aisle. Shelley's Walk beside the church commemorates a poem written in the churchyard during the poet's stay in 1815.

LITTLEDEAN

This village lies between Cinderford and Newnham. There are Norman pillars with shamrock carvings in the mainly thirteenth-century church. The prison at Littledean was a model prison designed by William Blackburn in 1785. Littledean Hall (chapter 5) is to the south of the village on the Newnham road.

LOWER and UPPER SLAUGHTER

The Slaughters are very busy in the tourist season. Both these pretty villages are in the valley of the Eye, a river which is spanned by footbridges as it runs between the neat stone cottages of Lower Slaughter. The mill (chapter 7) and a six-gabled dovecote are features at opposite ends of this village. The more hilly

Upper Slaughter.

Upper Slaughter has an Elizabethan manor house which is open at times. The church contains Norman work and a fourteenth-century sanctus bellcote. In the old parsonage the Reverend Francis Witts wrote *The Diary of a Cotswold Parson.*

LOWER and UPPER SWELL

These two charming Cotswold villages lie in the valley of the Dikler, just west of Stow-on-the-Wold. Lower Swell has good Norman carvings in the church and a war memorial designed by Sir Edwin Lutyens, who also designed the Cenotaph in Whitehall. Upper Swell, with its small church and mill, can be reached by a footpath beside the river Dikler. The brewery and fish farm at Donnington are just upstream (chapters 7 and 8).

LYDNEY

On the southern edge of the Forest of Dean, Lydney was once important for its iron industries and coal shipping. It is a good centre for exploring the Forest of Dean and other attractions, including the Lydney Park Gardens, museum, hillfort and Roman temple (chapters 5, 6 and 3), the Norchard Steam Centre of the Dean Forest Railway (chapter 8), and the

Egypt Mill, Nailsworth.

Lydney Harbour and Canal (chapter 7).

MINCHINHAMPTON

The High Street has houses with a good mixture of architectural styles from the sixteenth to eighteenth centuries. Beside two open triangles at the top end, the seventeenth-century Market Hall is supported on stone and wooden pillars. The church (Holy Trinity) has a truncated spire with small pinnacles. To the west, there are panoramic views from Minchinhampton Common, which was given to the village by Dame Alice Hampton in the sixteenth century and is now owned by the National Trust. There are several ancient earthworks here (chapters 2 and 3). Across the large common is **Amberley,** where Mrs Craik wrote the novel *John Halifax, Gentleman.*

MORETON-IN-MARSH
Early closing Wednesday.

A busy stopping place on the Fosse Way, Moreton-in-Marsh was once at the meeting of four counties; the Four Shire Stone is 1 mile (1.6 km) east on the A44. The town is high up on the Cotswolds, the 'marsh' in the name being derived from 'march', meaning boundary. Coaching inns along the broad High Street include the White Hart and the Redesdale Arms. In the centre of the street, the Redesdale Hall or Market Hall of 1887 has a tall clock-tower. On the corner with Oxford Street is the stone Curfew Tower with a bell dated 1633. The town lock-up is beneath and a board details the market tolls of 1905. The church (St David) is mostly of the nineteenth century and has a tower with spire 116 feet (35 metres) high. The Wellington Aviation Museum and Art Gallery (chapter 6) is in Broadway Road.

NAILSWORTH

The sides of a deep valley support the terraced cottages of textile workers who once staffed the mills which clustered in the valley bottom all the way to Stroud. Egypt Mill is now a restaurant, while Dunkirk Mill has been converted to flats (chapter 7). The Nailsworth Ladder has a gradient of about 1 in 2 and is known for motor trials. Steep lanes climb to **Box** village, which has good views over the valley. Minchinhampton Common is beyond (chapters 2 and 3).

NAUNTON

The village follows one long street in the sheltered Windrush valley and its setting is

The Market House, Newent.

best appreciated from the surrounding hills. The church stands in a large churchyard at the west end. Although much restored in 1899, it retains a small Saxon cross, a font and a stone pulpit of about 1400. Opposite the village hall is a restored four-gabled dovecote of about 1660, once belonging to a manor house which has vanished. **Guiting Power** and **Temple Guiting** are neat Cotswold villages further up the valley. The former has a small green and a church with a Norman south doorway and interesting corbel heads in the nave. The Cotswold Farm Park (chapter 8) is nearby, on the high ground above the valley.

NEWENT
Early closing Wednesday.
This is the main centre of the Vale of Leadon. Several black and white timber-framed buildings make a contrast to the mostly brick houses. These include the Tudor Fish and Chip Shop (1465) at the corner of Broad Street and Culver Street, and the Market House in the Market Square. The church (St Mary) has a notable spire. The nave was rebuilt by Edward Taylor after the roof collapsed in 1673. Saxon carvings point to an early foundation. Church Street also has the George Hotel (about 1649) and the Shambles Museum of Victorian Life (chapter 6). The Glassbarn is beside Tan House in Culver Street, the Newent Butterfly and Natural World Centre is in Birches Lane, while other attractions in the district are the

National Birds of Prey Centre and the Three Choirs Vineyard (chapter 8). To the east, **Upleadon**'s church has a notable timber and brick tower of about 1500.

NEWNHAM
This small town and former port is on the west bank of the great horseshoe bend of the Severn and is one of the gateways to the Forest of Dean from the A48. The main road passes through the tree-lined High Street, which has pleasant Georgian houses at the lower end near a stone clock-tower of 1875. There is a narrow park beside the Severn and from here Church Road leads round to the much restored church at the top of the High Street. There is a view from the churchyard across the Severn to the Vale of Berkeley. Gloucester's City Museum (chapter 6) contains the Newnham Sword, traditionally given to the town by King John. It is, however, of late fifteenth-century date, so it may have replaced an earlier sword.

NORTHLEACH
Early closing Thursday.
Established as a market town in the early thirteenth century by Gloucester Abbey, Northleach flourished for around three hundred years as a centre of the wool trade, as shown by its fine church (chapter 4). The triangular Market Place is surrounded by mostly Cotswold-stone houses. Some are half-timbered, such as the Red Lion Inn. In the Green, another is the Tudor House, which is reputed to have been the home of the wool merchant John Fortey. The church stands above and apart from the town, and below is the river Leach and a millpond for a mill which is now a house. This is Mill End, the oldest part of Northleach, where the Allen's Almshouses can be seen. The Dutton Almshouses are at East End. Just off the Market Place, in West End, Walton House is named after the racehorse son of a famous Derby winner. Keith Harding's World of Mechanical Music is in the High Street, and the Cotswold Countryside Collection in the House of Correction is at a crossroads on the Fosse Way (chapter 6).

PAINSWICK
Early closing Saturday.
Painswick is a hillside wool town full of charm, hidden from Gloucester by the crest of the Cotswold scarp. The houses are of local Painswick stone, which was also used for building Gloucester Cathedral. The main A46

*The market cross,
Stow-on-the-Wold.*

road follows the narrow New Street, avoiding the even narrower streets in the town centre. Bisley Street has some of the oldest houses, where arched doorways were for packhorses carrying bales of fleece and cloth. The Little Fleece Bookshop, owned by the National Trust, was part of the fourteenth-century Fleece Inn. Notable houses built for the Loveday family are Yew Tree House and Dover House (1720) in Vicarage Street and Loveday House in St Mary's Street. At the end of the latter, Court House (1600) was the home of Dr John Seaman, whose tomb is in the nearby church. The church and churchyard are full of interest (chapter 4), and the ancient Clipping Ceremony takes place on the Sunday nearest 19th September, when the singing choir and parishioners encircle the church. The special clipping hymn is sung, there are garlands of flowers and the children receive a free bun. Painswick had several mills, such as Painswick Mill for cloth at the bottom of Knap Lane. Savory's Mill at the bottom of Tibbiwell was the last to work, having been in turn a cloth, corn and pin mill since the fifteenth century. It has been converted to housing. Just north, up Gloucester Street, is the Painswick Rococo Garden (chapter 5).

SAPPERTON

The village is in a delightful setting 5 miles (8 km) west of Cirencester and overlooking the Frome or Golden Valley. The north portal of the Thames and Severn Canal's Sapperton Tunnel is far below (chapter 7). In the church-

yard of St Kenelm's church (chapter 4) lie buried Ernest Gimson and the brothers Ernest and Sidney Barnsley, architects and furniture makers of the Arts and Crafts Movement inspired by William Morris. They established their Cotswold workshops at Daneway House in the 1890s. They designed some of the houses in the village and elsewhere, such as Rodmarton Manor. Daneway House dates back to the fourteenth and seventeenth centuries and is open by written appointment only. John Masefield, the Poet Laureate, once lived further up the valley at Pinbury Park.

SHERBORNE

Most of Sherborne is a planned village of the early nineteenth century. Eleven rows of cottages extend for about a mile (1.6 km) on the south side of the Sherborne Brook, a tributary of the Windrush. They belong to the estate of Sherborne Park, which was owned by Winchcombe Abbey until the Dissolution, when it came to the Dutton family. The house of 1850 has been converted to flats, but the National Trust owns the park and woods, through which there are waymarked paths.

STANTON

The village is said to be the most perfect in the Cotswolds, its cottages and houses built in golden local stone and restored by the architect Sir Philip Stott in the years before the First World War. St Michael's church has a thin spire, twelfth-century features and fragments of stained glass from Hailes Abbey in the east window. A rare wooden pulpit of 1375 is now a lectern. The rood screen, two outer lights in the east window and the churchyard cross are First World War memorials designed by Sir Ninian Comper. John Wesley is said to have preached in the church and from the steps of the village cross.

STOW-ON-THE-WOLD
Early closing Wednesday.

At 750 feet (230 metres), Stow is the highest town in the Cotswolds and can be cold and windy. A market grew up here at the meeting of eight roads and the town became a busy wool town. Daniel Defoe recorded twenty thousand sheep for sale at an annual fair in 1724. Today, the town is a busy tourist centre off the Fosse Way. The large Market Square is surrounded by period houses and coaching inns. At the south end is the market cross with a restored lantern head, while the stocks are on the Green at the other end. In the centre, the tall Victorian St Edward's Hall is now the library. In a niche over the door is a statue of King Edward the Confessor. Off the Square, the Tures are narrow sheep alleys leading to

Church House, Stroud, from St Lawrence's churchyard.

other streets. Digbeth Street descends to the wide Park Street, while Church Street leads to Sheep Street, which has galleries, antique shops and a development in the old brewery yard where Chantry House is an unusual office. The large church (St Edward) dates from Norman times with later work of the thirteenth to fifteenth centuries. It was much ruined when a thousand captured Royalists were imprisoned in it after one of the last battles of the Civil War. The Stow Wells, once an important source of water, are along Well Lane.

STROUD
Early closing Thursday; market day Saturday.

At a meeting of valleys surrounded by hills of the Cotswold edge, Stroud was the centre of the broadcloth industry and produced famous dyes such as the scarlet used for military uniforms. Special cloths for uniforms and for covering billiard tables and tennis balls are finished and dyed here today at Lodgemore Mill. The buildings of eighteenth- and nineteenth-century woollen mills still stand, many turned to other uses (see chapter 7). The wealth brought by the industry is reflected in some of the architecture around the town. The handsome Subscription Rooms building faces a square in George Street. It was built in the neo-classical style in 1833 by Charles Baker, who completed the fine Bedford Street Congregational Chapel (1837) next door. Behind, and across the High Street, the Shambles was the old meat market, where John Wesley once preached. The Town Hall of 1594 faces a long colonnade here. The church (St Lawrence) stands at the end, rebuilt in 1866, except the fourteenth-century tower. The museum and industrial collection (chapter 6) are worth visiting in Lansdown. The former is in the impressive School of Science and Art, built in 1890-9. Rowcroft has some good late eighteenth-century houses and a statue of Henry Holloway, clothier and founder of the first benefit society. Under the railway bridge and beyond is the junction of the Stroudwater Canal and Thames and Severn Canal (chapter 7). Each year, the Stroud Show is held in July and the Stroud and District Festival in October. Just to the north-west is **Randwick**, where a cheese-rolling ceremony is held in May. To the north-east, the B4070 follows the Slad valley, where the scattered village of **Slad** was immortalised by Laurie Lee's autobiographical *Cider with Rosie.*

73

The Market House, Tetbury.

TETBURY

Early closing Thursday; market day Wednesday.

A south Cotswolds town of some charm, Tetbury has many antique and other interesting shops. In the centre the robust Market House of 1665 stands on three rows of stone pillars. Long Street has Georgian stone houses, and at the end the Old Police Station and Courthouse has a museum (chapter 6) and a tourist information centre. The old stone-built brewery remains a prominent architectural feature in Hampton Street, which leads towards the Elizabethan manor at Chavenage (chapter 5). The Chipping is off Chipping Lane and was once the livestock market but is now a car park. The picturesque cobbled Chipping Steps descend from this square. Gumstool Hill is another old street. Here, competitors race with heavy sacks of wool on Woolsack Day, which is held on Spring Bank Holiday Monday in late May, when there is also a street fair. Along Church Street, the architecture of the church with its tall spire is not to be missed (chapter 4).

TEWKESBURY

Early closing Thursday; market days Wednesday and Saturday.

Tewkesbury is a busy market town at the confluence of the Severn and Avon rivers, surrounded by a low-lying district subject to flooding. In the late sixteenth century it was famous for woollen cloth and mustard, but the corn trade later became important by utilising river transport on the Severn so that today the working Borough or Healing's flour mill is a prominent feature in Quay Street. Tewkesbury presents one of the best medieval townscapes in England, with good timbered houses, dominated by the tower of the large Norman abbey church (chapter 4). There are several hostelries of note. In Church Street, the Bell Hotel, a guest house for the abbey, has associations with Mrs Craik's *John Halifax, Gentleman*, while the Royal Hop Pole Hotel appears in Charles Dickens's *Pickwick Papers*. In the High Street, the Tudor House Hotel was built in 1540, the Ancient Grudge owes its name to the Wars of the Roses, and the timber-framed Old Black Bear at the junction with Mythe Road could date from 1308. In contrast is the classical stone façade of the Town Hall. There are three museums in Tewkesbury (chapter 6). The Town Museum is in an early seventeenth-century timber-framed building (also the tourist information centre) in Barton Street, while the Little Museum and John Moore Countryside Museum are in an attractive row of fifteenth-century houses in Church Street.

Winchcombe.

Opposite these, a narrow alley leads to the restored Baptist Chapel, a timber-framed building of 1690 with later furnishings and three galleries. Nearby, the short Mill Street ends at the Abbey Mill (chapter 7), with a footbridge beside the sluices to the Severn Ham, an island of meadow land owned by the town; the grass is auctioned each year. To the south of the abbey, Lincoln Green Lane leads off Gloucester Road to Bloody Meadow, the site of a bloody battle on 4th May 1471 when Edward IV's Yorkists defeated Queen Margaret of Anjou's Lancastrian forces, who were led by the Duke of Somerset. There is a waymarked battle trail across the area. The Tewkesbury Mop Fair dates from the eleventh century and is held in October when there is a fair and market in the streets.

WINCHCOMBE
Early closing Thursday.

An attractive small town in the valley of the river Isbourne, Winchcombe is surrounded by hills except to the north. It was the Saxon capital of Mercia, where a nunnery was first founded in AD 787, and a monastery soon after. Within, the shrine of the young martyred prince Kenelm became a centre of pilgrimage. The abbey was dissolved on Christmas Eve 1539 and demolished soon afterwards. A cross marks the site of the high altar in a private garden off Abbey Terrace just east of the church. As well as pilgrims, the abbey also brought wealth from sheep and the wool trade. Jack Smallwood, who made Winchcombe jerseys, was the Jack O'Newbury who paid for three hundred men to fight at Flodden Field in 1513. The old fulling mill became a silk mill for a short period, while paper is still made upstream at Postlip Mill. Tobacco was grown in the district for a while in the seventeenth century.

Many of the town's houses are of local stone, with a few timbered examples. At the junction of the High Street and North Street, the Tudor-style Town Hall dates from 1871. It contains the tourist information centre and a small museum upstairs (chapter 6). The old George Inn opposite was a pilgrims' hostel with a galleried courtyard but has been converted to flats. To the west, the High Street broadens at Abbey Terrace, with the good stone Jacobean House facing Queen's Square at the end. St Peter's church in Gloucester Street was built in 1465-8 and has been little altered since. Pinnacles and crenellations adorn the tower, nave and south porch. Around forty grotesques and gargoyles, the 'Winchcombe Worthies', are said to represent unpopular monks and give an indication of how the town

75

resented the abbey's power. Inside, the chancel is continuous with the tall clerestoried nave beneath timbered ceilings. An embroidery is dated 1380-90, with a border traditionally attributed to Katherine of Aragon. The supposed stone coffin of St Kenelm is also in the church. The fascinating Winchcombe Railway Museum (chapter 6) is along the curving Gloucester Street, and on the corner with Malthouse Lane the buttressed Corner Cupboard Inn was originally a Tudor farmhouse. Sudeley Castle (chapter 5), the home of Katherine Parr, is just to the south-east, the Belas Knap long barrow (chapter 3) stands on a hill 1½ miles (2 km) to the south, while Hailes Abbey (chapter 5), the Winchcombe Pottery and Gloucestershire-Warwickshire Railway (chapter 8) are north of the town.

WOTTON-UNDER-EDGE
Early closing Wednesday.

This is a hillside town in an attractive setting, with a good variety of houses and architectural styles. The main shops are down the High Street, which becomes Long Street at the junction with Market Street. On the corner here is the Tolsey House, with a copper dragon weather-vane on a cupola and a projecting clock of 1897. Market Street ends at the Market Square and Town Hall. Halfway down Long Street, Berkeley House has a stone Jacobean front. Terraced houses in Orchard Street (off Long Street) include the house where Isaac Pitman invented his phonography method of shorthand in 1837. The modern library at the top of Ludgate Hill contains a small museum (chapter 6). Church Street has the Perry and Dawes Almshouses around a quadrangle with a small chapel. The oldest parts, including the chapel, were endowed in 1638 by Hugh Perry, while Thomas Dawe's additions date from the 1720s. The church (St Mary) has a fine tower and spacious interior. Memorials include the early fourteenth-century table tomb and brasses of Thomas, Lord Berkeley (who fought at Agincourt), and his wife, Lady Margaret. It was Katherine, Lady Berkeley, who founded an early grammar school nearby in the 1380s. At the top of the town, up Tabernacle Road, are the Reverend Rowland Hill's striking Tabernacle Church and group of almshouses.

To the north-west of Wotton stands the Tyndale Monument at **North Nibley** (chapter 2). To the south lies the village of **Kingswood**, with its old abbey gateway (chapter 5). **Alderley** is to the south-east, on the county border with Avon. Sir Matthew Hale was born here at The Grange in 1609 and became a famous judge and chief justice in the Commonwealth and Restoration periods. He was devout but obsessed with witchcraft. Newark Park (chapter 5) is 1½ miles (2 km) to the east.

'Worthies' carved on the parish church at Winchcombe.

The Perry and Dawes Almshouses, Wotton-under-Edge.

10
Tourist information centres

Cheltenham: 77 The Promenade, Cheltenham GL50 1PP. Telephone: 0242 522878.

Chipping Campden*: Woolstaplers Hall Museum, High Street, Chipping Campden GL55 6HB. Telephone: 0386 840289.

Cinderford: The Library, Belle Vue Road, Cinderford GL14 2BX. Telephone: 0594 823184.

Cirencester: Corn Hall, Market Place, Cirencester GL7 2NW. Telephone: 0285 654180.

Coleford: Council Offices, Market Place, Coleford GL16 8HG. Telephone: 0594 36307.

Gloucester: St Michael's Tower, The Cross, Gloucester GL1 1PD. Telephone: 0452 421188.

Newent: The Library, High Street, Newent GL18 1AN. Telephone: 0531 822145.

Northleach*: Cotswold Countryside Collection, Fosseway, Northleach GL54 3JH. Telephone: 0451 60715.

Painswick: The Library, Stroud Road, Painswick GL6 6UT. Telephone: 0452 813552.

Stow-on-the-Wold: Talbot Court, off Sheep Street, Stow-on-the-Wold GL54 1BQ. Telephone: 0451 31082.

Stroud: Subscription Rooms, Kendrick Street, Stroud GL5 1AE. Telephone: 0453 765768.

Tetbury*: The Old Court House, 63 Long Street, Tetbury GL8 8AA. Telephone: 0666 53552.

Tewkesbury: The Museum, Barton Street, Tewkesbury GL20 5PX. Telephone: 0684 295027.

Winchcombe*: Town Hall, High Street, Winchcombe GL54 5LJ. Telephone: 0242 602925.

* Seasonal opening only.

GLOUCESTERSHIRE

KEY

✳ Countryside (Ch.2)
⊓ Places of archaeological interest (Ch.3)
✚ Church (Ch.4)
▲ Historic building or garden (Ch.5)
M Museum or gallery (Ch.6)
I Industrial archaeology (Ch.7)
○ Other places to visit (Ch.8)
■ Town or village (Ch.9)
● Other villages

Dymock ■

Deerhurst ✚

*Three Choirs
Vineyards* ○

R. Leadon

Coombe
Cana

Upleadon ●

○■ **M**
Newent

Ashleworth
Tithe Barn ▲

R. Severn

○ *National Birds
of Prey Centre*

Nature in Art
M

✳ *May Hill*

Highnam Woods ✳

*Over
Bridge* **I**

✚
■■ GLOUCES
M⊓

Llanthony Priory

Gloucester and Sharpness Canal

Robinswood
✳ *Hill* Co
○

*Symonds
Yat Rock* ✳

✚ *English
Bicknor*

*Shapridge Guns
Mills Furnace*
⊓ *Welshbury Camp*

Prinknash Abbey▲

Painswick ⊓
Beacon

CINDERFORD ■

■ *Littledean*

▲ *Westbury
Court
Garden*

*Painswick Roco
Garden* ▲

R. Wye

*Speech House
Woodland* ✳ **I**

*Lightmoor
Colliery* **I**

*Blaize
Bailey*

■ *Newnham*

Painswick ⊓
✚

Longstone ⊓

COLEFORD ■**M**
I

*Cannop
Valley*

*Soudley
Ponds* ✳
M

*Bullo
Pill* **I**

*Haresfield
Beacon* ✳⊓

*Whitecliff
Furnace* ■**M**

Slad ⊓

Redbrook ●
Newland ■

✚

○ *Puzzle
Wood*

✳ *New
Fancy*

*Dean
Heritage Centre*

● *Randwick*

*Clearwell
Caves*

Clearwell ■

*Nagshead
Nature Reserve*

I *Park End
engine house*

Blackpool Bridge
⊓

Frampton-
on-Severn ■

M■ STR

Offa's Dyke
✳ ⊓

■ *Bream*

*Wildfowl and
Wetlands
Centre* ○

I Ebley Mill
✚ Selsley

St

▲ *St Briavels
Castle*

*Dean Forest
Railway* ○

Stanley Mill **I**

*Minchinhampton
Common* ✳

✚
Hewelsfield

⊓▲
Lydney ■**M**
Park

■ LYDNEY

Frocester Tithe Barn ▲

Coaley Peak ✳⊓

▲ *Woodchester
Park Mansion* *Minchinha*

*Lydney
Harbour* **I**

Sharpness ■

*Hetty Pegler's
Tump* ⊓

I *Dunk
Mill*

*Wintour's
Leap* ✳

M■ *Berkeley*
▲

○ *Uley Bury*

DURSLEY ■

Uley ⊓

NAILSWORTH

Berkeley Castle

Uley ●

*Tyndale
Monument* ✳

*Brackenbury
Ditches* ⊓

Chavenage ▲

*Wotton-under-
Edge* **M**■

▲ *Newark Park*

TETBU

New Mill ▲

*Kingswood
Abbey Gatehouse*

Alderley ●

*Westonbirt
Arboretum*

⊓ *Nan Tow's
Tump*

Index

Page numbers in italic refer to illustrations.